EDUCATION AND DEVELOPMENT IN LATIN AMERICA

EDUCATION AND DEVELOPMENT IN LATIN AMERICA

With special reference to Columbia and some comparison with Guyana, South America

LAURENCE GALE

Volume 60

Routledge
Taylor & Francis Group

LONDON AND NEW YORK

First published in 1969

This edition first published in 2011
by Routledge
2 Park Square, Milton Park, Abingdon, Oxon, OX14 4RN

Simultaneously published in the USA and Canada
by Routledge
270 Madison Avenue, New York, NY 10016

Routledge is an imprint of the Taylor & Francis Group, an informa business

© 1969 Laurence Gale

British Library Cataloguing in Publication Data
A catalogue record for this book is available from the British Library

ISBN 13: 978-0-415-58414-2 (Set)
eISBN 13: 978-0-203-84035-1 (Set)
ISBN 13: 978-0-415-59461-5 (Volume 60)
eISBN 13: 978-0-203-83750-4 (Volume 60)

Publisher's Note
The publisher has gone to great lengths to ensure the quality of this reprint but
points out that some imperfections in the original copies may be apparent.

Disclaimer
The publisher has made every effort to trace copyright holders and welcomes
correspondence from those they have been unable to contact.

Education and Development in Latin America

With special reference to Colombia and some comparison with Guyana, South America

LAURENCE GALE

London
ROUTLEDGE & KEGAN PAUL

First published in 1969
by Routledge & Kegan Paul Limited
Broadway House, 68–74 Carter Lane
London, E.C.4
Printed in Great Britain by
Richard Clay (The Chaucer Press), Ltd.,
Bungay, Suffolk
© *Laurence Gale, 1969*

SBN 7100 6398 9

Contents

Map   viii

World education series   ix

General editor's introduction   xiii

Acknowledgments   xiv

PART ONE

1 Introduction: Privilege and deprivation   3
A tradition of submission   7
The experience of violence   9
Town and country   10

2 The legal basis, policy and finance   14
The administration of education   15
Educational reform   20
Financial planning   23
Priorities   25

3 The primary school   28
Universal enrolment   29
School building   32
The quality of primary education   34
Research and experiment   35
Rural pilot projects   37
Radio and television   39
Teachers   41
The training of teachers   43
The status of teachers   45

4 The secondary stage   46
Private secondary schools   47
The traditional curriculum   49

Contents

Reform   50
Vocational education   53
Obstacles to progress   58
The supply and training of teachers   60
Radio and television   61
Motives and priorities   63

5 Higher education   65
Growth of technical studies   67
Vocational and liberal education   70
The university and the community   73
Research   76
University reform   77
Financing of higher education   79
Student participation in university affairs   80
Student enrolment   82
Standards   84
University staff   86

PART TWO

6 The forming of opinion and the role of education   91
The impact of technology   91
Urban life   96
The spirit of revolt   97
Revolutionary change   102
The debate continues   104
The influence of the teaching profession   107
International organizations   109
La Educación   113

PART THREE

7 Adult education and community development   117
Basic and community education   118
The radio schools movement   123
Rural development and education   127

Contents

8 Overseas aid and education   131
   International experts   134
   Study abroad   136
   Education and manpower requirements   141

9 The Colombian balance sheet   147
   The primary school   149
   Higher education   152
   Secondary schools   158
   The old and the new worlds   160
   Education, revolution and reform   164

Bibliography   166

Further Reading   169

U. S. A.
MEXICO
Monterrey
Mexico City
BRITISH HONDURAS
GUATEMALA
EL SALVADOR
HONDURAS
NICARAGUA
COSTA RICA
PANAMA
Barranquilla
Cartagena
Caracas
Ciudad Guyana
VENEZUELA
Georgetown
SURINAM
FR GUIANA
Medellin
Bogota
Cali
COLOMBIA
Quito
ECUADOR
Guayaquil
Manaous
Amazon
PERU
BRAZIL
Lima
Arequipa
La Paz
BOLIVIA
Oruro
Brasilia
Rio de Janeiro
Sao Paulo
PARAGUAY
URUGUAY
Cordoba
Rosario
Valparaiso
Santiago
CHILE
Concepción
Buenos Aires
Punta del Este
Montevideo
ARGENTINA

World education series

The volumes in the *World Education Series* will treat national systems of education and, where appropriate, features of different systems within a particular region. These studies are intended to meet the needs of students of comparative education in university departments and schools of education and colleges of education and will supplement the growing volume of literature in the field. They may also appeal to a wider lay audience interested in education abroad.

As an area study of a national system each volume presents an accurate, reasonably up-to-date account of the most important features of the educational system described. Among these are the ways in which the school system is controlled, financed and administered. Some account is given of the various kinds of school within the system and the characteristics of each of them. The principles of curriculum organization and some aspects of teacher education are outlined. Of more interest, however, is the analysis which is made in each volume of the unique national characteristics of an educational system, seen in the context of its history and the sociological, economic and political factors which have in the past and continue now to influence educational policy.

The assumption behind the series is, however, that common socio-economic and educational problems find unique expression in a particular country or region, and that a brief analysis of some major national issues will reveal similarities and differences. Thus, while in each case the interpretation of policies and practices is based on the politics of education, the interpretative emphasis will vary from one country to another.

The framework of analysis for each volume is consequently the same, attention being drawn in the first section to the legal basis of educational provision, followed in the second section by an analysis of the political considerations which have and do influence the formulation, adoption and implementation of policy. The role of political parties is described where appropriate and the influence of the church or churches on policy examined. Attention too is given to the activities of pressure groups at national, regional and local levels. Changing industrial, urban and familial patterns are used to show how educational needs are in process of change and what difficulties arise when innovations are attempted. Again, each author touches on the extent to which economic resources affect the implementation of policy. The analysis relates principally to the twenty-year period between 1945 and 1965 but relevant aspects of the pre-Second World War period are described and the chains of events are seen in historical perspective.

Finally, in the third section some account is given of problems which arise within the educational system itself. Those which appear to the author of particular interest and importance have been treated in some depth. Others have been referred to so that readers may consult other sources of information if they wish. Broad problem areas in education have, however, been identified. The points of transition within a system between the first and second and between the second and third stages of education give rise to problems of selection and allocation. Under conditions of expansion, created by explosions of population and aspirations, traditional solutions are often thought to be no longer adequate. The attempts made to meet these new situations are described. So too are the relationships and debates about them, between the various types of school at different levels of education. For example what are the possibilities of transfer between academic, general and technical/ vocation schools at the second stage of education? And where these different types have been replaced by some form of common or comprehensive school what kinds of differentiation exist within the single school? At the third level of higher education what relationships exist between institutions providing general education, professional training and research opportunities? In some systems a form of dual control is growing up with the universities retaining much of their traditional autonomy and the technological institutes and teacher education institutions increasingly feeling the influence of government agencies. Again, after a process of differentiation in course content in the first stage of higher education there is now a tendency for the first year (or two) of college or university work to be regarded as a preparatory year (or years) with common or somewhat similar courses of studies for all students.

Particular attention has been paid to the problems which arise in the area of teacher education. Movements in most countries are in the direction of bringing together the previously separate systems of training for elementary and secondary school teachers. Common entrance prerequisites to different training institutions may now be required. Where this is not yet the case training colleges usually make it possible for students to obtain, during the course of their studies, a certificate which grants entry to the university and highest (in prestige and status) forms of teacher education. The place of teacher education in the structure of higher education is, in short, discussed in each of the volumes. So are debates about curricular content and methods of certification.

Finally, some attention is given to the interaction of the schools and other social agencies. Among these the health services, youth organizations, the family, the Church, industry and commerce have been regarded as important. Where special note is not taken of such institutions the impact they have in the schools is dealt with throughout the volume as a whole.

The framework in short is intended to facilitate cross cultural studies through the series as a whole. Basic educational legislation is referred to in the belief that it gives the most reliable and valid source of national goals or aims in education. The problems of putting these into effective action are socio-economic-political and educational. Comparisons can be made, therefore, between the aims of education as expressed in national legislation and between the main factors which inhibit or facilitate practical provisions in accordance with these aims.

BRIAN HOLMES
General Editor

General editor's introduction

In this volume Mr Gale has surveyed some problems which arise in Latin American countries in the belief that even though solutions to them may differ somewhat from one country to another the conditions in which they arise are sufficiently similar to make comparisons possible and useful. After describing the uneven provision of schools for different sections of the community as characteristic of all Latin American countries, Mr Gale goes on to point out that the peoples of Latin America are not homogeneous and have never felt themselves to be one people. In the course of time the races and cultures have intermingled but even so the continent is still a confusion of languages and cultures with great differences in climate and terrain, between social classes, between the rich and the poor, and between rural and urban dwellers. Against this background of diversity Mr Gale examines common features in education throughout Latin America, areas of co-operation and agreement, and differences of policy and provision. He draws heavily on illustrative material from Colombia which he knows well, having worked there for several years.

BRIAN HOLMES

Acknowledgments

I gratefully acknowledge the help which I have received from many friends in Latin America and in Britain while I have been writing this book. I am particularly indebted to Meyer Sasson, Melvin Hughes, Hermilo Lopez Bassols, Jorge Piñol and Anne Murray. They are not, however, in any way responsible for the accuracy of the text or for the opinions expressed. I am also grateful to my wife and to Miss Carol Soper for helping me with typing.

PART ONE

After sketching the general background to the educational problems facing the South American continent Part One describes the legal and financial basis of the educational systems, and the main characteristics of the primary, secondary and higher sectors.

Introduction: Privilege and deprivation

The wise Colombian child would choose his parents with care. If his father were one of the herdsmen of the subtropical plains which slope down to the Orinoco basin from the eastern cordillera of the Andes his chance of going to school would be remote, though it would exist if he lived near one of the scattered mission stations. It would be little better if he were born in a poverty-stricken village of the arid mountains of the Guajira peninsula which thrusts itself into the Caribbean on the borders of Venezuela, or in the hot valleys of the Choco which carry the heaviest downpours of Colombia to the Pacific. Antioqueñian parents would be at a great advantage, for the pioneering spirit and hard work of the people of Antioquia have played an effective role in the development of the country: they appreciate the value of education. The coffee gardens of Caldas, the main source of wealth of the country, can afford schools; so too can the valley of the Cauca, an even carpet of tropical crops and pasture stretching to the very slopes of the mountains. Most favoured is the child of the plain of Bogotá whose temperate fields and meadows are reminiscent of Scotland, or France or Switzerland, fertile and intensely farmed. As this brief survey suggests, the disparity of educational opportunity in Colombia is so extreme that the schools in different regions do not fit easily into one national system.

The same uneven provision of schools is characteristic of all Latin American countries. In Portuguese-speaking Brazil the children of the south-eastern states, with the cities of Rio de Janeiro and São Paulo, are privileged as compared with those of the north-east, while these again are far better provided for than the children of the forests of the north and west.

Similarly, in Peru the Indians of the 'altiplano', 10,000 feet up in the Andes, growing just enough potatoes to live on, fall sadly behind the inhabitants of the irrigated valleys of the Pacific coast in their schooling, and especially behind the area around the capital where most of the social services of the country are concentrated.

The position is much the same in the former British territory, Guyana. While each coastal village has its school, in the interior, where the only means of local communication is by river and creek, the schools are scattered and only within the reach of children living no more than an hour or two's boat journey away.

The differences of educational opportunity reflect differences in the physical characteristics of the regions and countries of the continent. Colombia is typical, a land of startling contrasts. If you go by road from the capital, Bogotá, which lies on a plateau at 8,500 feet, you drop abruptly down the side of the cordillera, twisting and turning until you come to the plain of the Magdelena River. You have left behind the temperate highlands, almost European in appearance with their fields of wheat and potatoes, their apples and pears and strawberries, their grazing Frisian and Jersey cattle, and their solid houses. You have passed through the orange groves and coffee gardens of the slopes. The road is now straight and on each side are level fields of sugar, maize and cotton, with clumps of banana trees clustered around the wooden homesteads. It is a hot and steaming land until shortly beyond the red muddy stream of the Magdelena where the road climbs again, winding upwards for 5,000 or 6,000 feet into the dark clouds. Beyond the crest of the central range you plunge down again and passing out of the mists of the high mountains you turn a corner and suddenly below stretches the valley of the Cauca, cultivated right up to the barren slopes of the foothills.

Whichever direction you take you will see changes equally abrupt. Go from Bogotá to the south, climbing still higher until you reach the páramos, the moors, desolate, cold, a perpetual Arctic spring. Or go eastwards down into the upper basins of the Orinoco and the Amazon, into the savannahs and the tropical jungle of the river-beds. Or fly by aeroplane to the coast, passing over vast areas of bare mountain and untracked forest to arrive at the modern city and port of Barranquilla on the Caribbean, or the walled city of Cartagena, the ancient gateway to the Indies. These physical obstacles have thwarted the efforts of successive governments to achieve the objective formally stated in the Constitution of creating a homo-geneous national outlook through education.

Beyond the frontiers of Colombia, throughout the Latin American countries, the contrasts are equally striking. In Argentina, Uruguay and Costa Rica, you would be remarkable if you did not learn to read and write at school. In Peru and Mexico, Ecuador, Paraguay and Brazil, you would have an even chance of learning to read, and indeed better than even if you were a town-dweller. In Bolivia, Guatemala, Honduras and Nicaragua, the skill of reading is the privilege of a minority. The contrasting patterns of educational opportunity reflects the physical differences between the countries. The Andes form a backbone of the countries to the south. In Ecuador and Peru the intermontane basins and gentle slopes of the high plateaux are surmounted by towering ranges, lined with the cones of volcanoes, Chimborazo and Cotapaxi and Huascarán. The eastern slopes of the Andes in Ecuador, Peru and Bolivia drop down to the Amazonian basin, a huge area of tropical forest and jungle, traversed only by rivers. In Argentina these slopes lead to the *pampas*, the level, green but treeless open spaces, so extensive that they have palm trees on their northern borders and touch on Antarctic glaciers and blizzards to the south. On the west the narrow coastal plain starts in Ecuador as swamp, becomes desert in Peru, and after pas-sing through the well-watered valleys of central Chile, breaks up into a labyrinth of fjords, creeks and islands at the southern tip of the continent. There is little in the physical make-up of the continent which would lead one to expect uniformity even in the provision of social services and schools. Against the background of varied physical features and human and economic development it is not surprising that some countries have been able to provide a good standard of general education for the majority of their people, while others fail to provide even the basic elements of instruction. At one end of the scale Argentina, with a homogeneous population who brought with them the cultural traditions and education of Europe, was able to take advantage of favourable marketing conditions dur-ing the nineteenth century to build up a prosperous economy and the resources necessary for an adequate educational system. At the other extreme, history and geography have been less kind to Guate-mala.

The contrasting patterns are accentuated because the peoples of

Latin America are not homogeneous. The indigenous inhabitants never felt themselves to be one people. Before the Europeans came the Aztecs of Mexico looked down on neighbouring tribes as uncivilized, speaking a barbaric language; they knew little of the Quechua Indians whose Inca empire also collapsed with the first arrival of a handful of Spaniards, and nothing of the Araucanians of Chile who permanently waged war on the fringes of the Spanish domains. Only the arbitrary name, Indian, mistakenly imposed on the aborigines of the New World by the conquerors gave these varied tribes a unity they never possessed. The European immigration equally lacked a common origin. In spite of the Papal Bull of 1493 which purported to reserve South America to the Spanish and Portuguese, over the centuries other European nations have joined those who came from the Iberian peninsula to seek a new life in the west. In Chile and the south-eastern states of Brazil, German and Italian colonization has produced vigorous agricultural communities, while in Argentina, Colombia, Chile and Peru the prevalence of Spanish-speaking families with English, Scots and Irish surnames is evidence of continuous contact, starting with participation in the black slave trade, and continued from the wars of independence against Spain through the century of railroad construction, mining and free trade. The Welsh recently celebrated the hundredth anniversary of their settlements in Patagonia. Around the tropical eastern coasts those who survived the forced journeys from Africa added rhythm and liveliness to the mixture of strains, and in Peru and the Central American States the Chinese brought with their spices the patient market and garden skills of the East. In Guyana the labourers of India and Sumatra came to toil among the sugar cane, and stayed to cultivate rice on their own plot, to trade in the markets and to set up their lawyer's sign.

In the course of time the races and cultures have intermingled, producing a wide variety of pigmentation and custom as the hazards of time and place determined. In Ecuador nearly half of the population are pure Amerindian, in Costa Rica the people are predominantly of Spanish stock. The impoverished descendants of the Quechua Incas still inhabit the highlands of Peru and Bolivia; Argentina is populated by people almost entirely of European origin. Something over half the people of Colombia, Chile, Paraguay, Honduras and Nicaragua are mestizos – Indians with some admixture of Spanish blood – while in Brazil the mulatto descendants of Negroes and whites amount to almost a third of the total numbers. Though the world thinks of the continent as Latin, this confusion of languages and cultures has not been blended into one harmonious South American whole.

A tradition of submission

When Colombus landed in the Americas the indigenous Indians had their own system of educating young men into the ways of the tribe. Indeed, schools were established by the Incas to train leaders (Mason, 1964), and in the Aztec empire no Mexican child went without some form of schooling, either for the priesthood or the high offices of state, or to become a warrior or an artisan (Soustelle, 1964). This was encouraging for those conquerors such as Las Casas who, after first seeking glory and gold, espoused the cause of the universal human spirit and of the Indians, and whose humanitarian mission was continued in later years by the teaching orders. The Jesuits were particularly active, covering the continent with schools and banishing illiteracy in those areas which came under their sway. To sustain education for the Indian, however, proved a forlorn cause. It was in the indigenous tradition to submit to superior authority, and this submissiveness was, if anything, pushed still further by the teaching of the Church that life is suffering which has no hope of relief on this earth. This 'other-worldliness' confirmed a reluctance to lift a finger in self help and offered no spur to seek education. Bruised in his soul by the conquest, the Indian accepted the *yanacona*, service in the household of the Spanish overlord, and the role of serf and peon on the great estates, the *encomiendas* which had been awarded, with their inhabitants and their produce, to important Spanish leaders as rewards for services. In isolated mountain valleys, Quechua or Guaraní, mestizo or mulatto, now wrests a poor livelihood from the soil, illiterate, deprived of the amenities of the modern industrial world and of schools, dependent upon the landlord and businessman. And still further in the remoteness of the tropical forest live the primitive peoples, such as the Barí, for example, the close-cropped ones, a tribe of the borders of Colombia and Venezuela, west of the Gulf of Maracaibo. For three centuries in intermittent contact with the outside world, they still maintain their traditional organization, in spite of recent civilizing efforts of the Capuchins, living in family groups in long houses, hunting and fishing, cultivating a little cassava, potatoes, banana and cotton, fearful of the ways of strangers, careless of schools. The picture is very different in those areas where the European predominates, though again the social benefits are not shared by the unprivileged. In all the countries of Latin America two worlds live side by side: an archaic world, medieval in character, in which the masses receive no more than the bare essentials of education, and the world of the privileged, often the white élite, who live much more in contact with the external world of culture than with the national population (Gomez Valderrama, 1964).

The pattern of settlement did not bring the different groups together. The civilizing mission lost ground before the greed of the conqueror and the demands of the developing industrial civilization of Europe and later of North America for primary products and minerals. For centuries the European invaders did not cease to look over their shoulders to Madrid and Lisbon, France and England, not only because Europe was the cultural heart of their world but increasingly because the cities of Europe were their source of capital and the markets for their produce. The settlements which were established were mainly on the coasts and looked outwards. Even though the legend of El Dorado together with the healthy climate and the promise of mineral wealth drew the settlers inland, until recently Bogotá, Quito and La Paz remained small colonial towns. The slow journey upstream in boats, even until this century propelled by the arms of men, and along mule tracks laboriously hacked through forest and out of the face of precipices, was an effective barrier to internal links. The Inca with their elaborate relay system along high mountain roads were more successful in maintaining communications than those who followed. The European settlements looked outwards over the sea, and each developed separately around its main product, coffee or tin, nitrates or bananas, petroleum or wool.

The experience of violence

Violence, a recurring feature of the history of the continent, has promoted the tendency towards fragmentation. The Spanish personality and the pattern of conquest made it inevitable that the man of action would play a decisive role. The four or five army dictatorships which exist today have their beginnings in the earliest period of occupation when the military rising, the *golpe* in the capital or provincial *pronunciamiento*, pretended to sweep away bad government in the name of the king or of the republic. At the same time the bitterness which festered in the minds of the disgruntled and the wronged burst out into violence, impeding the emergence of stable social and political conditions where education could thrive. Schooling was a rare privilege which had to be jealously kept as a safeguard against prevailing uncertainty. Colombia, the scene of Bolívar's ultimate victory at Boyacá, certainly typifies this spirit of revolt, and in spite of the claim of Bogotá to be the Athens of South America, can offer examples of violence unsurpassed in horror. The civil war of 1899 counted one hundred thousand dead, and in the twenty years after 1946, when the killings started anew, there were reported to be two hundred thousand victims (Guzman, Uñana, Fals Borda, 1962). The recent period of bloody conflict started with the murder in the centre of Bogotá of the progressive political leader Jorge Elieser Gaitán. This death stopped abruptly the chances of progressive leadership and reform. It led to rural unrest, countered by repressive action by government forces, which in its turn was followed by a declaration of civic resistance by the Liberal Party. Before long what started as a struggle between parties rushed headlong out of control of the leaders of either side. Without understanding the political issues, men killed with machete and gun, sometimes to pay off old scores, or even just for the sake of killing. They fought for no cause, and without vision of a better world (Deas, 1965). Violence became a vested interest benefiting some politicians, the bandits themselves and landless peasants who had acquired empty estates. It made necessary the maintenance of a large army and police force, absorbing resources which could have been used more fruitfully for development. It might also be suggested that the alliance between the Conservative and Liberal

Parties, which made it possible to bring the violence under some control, led to atrophy of ideas and unwillingness to experiment. Alarmed by that prodigious letting of blood, the politicians avoided any conflict of ideas lest it led to a fresh outbreak.

Nevertheless, the *violencia* in Colombia and in other states had effects not necessarily disastrous. It accelerated the breakaway from the paternalism of the Church and rural landlord. It led to the emergence of secular organization in which the school and the library came before the church. It also contributed to changes in circumstances which must ultimately lead Colombians to revise their traditional attitudes. It called accepted authority to account and posed the urgent necessity for planning and reform, just as earlier in the century the Mexican revolution cut away much of the dead wood of the past and prepared the way for new growth (Fals Borda, 1965). The experience of violence pointed with particular emphasis to the need for more provision for education in the rural areas not only to lead people to seek other solutions to their differences but also to provide the means for them to develop and meet the demands of rising population.

Town and country

The insecurity of the rural areas in Colombia was one of the reasons for the movement of people from the country to the towns, though, of course, the improvement of transport, higher standards of living and better services and education in the towns, and the attraction of industrial employment and more favourable labour legislation were also factors. Since 1938 the town of Cali has multiplied its population five times, and Bogotá, Medellin and Bucaramanga more than three times. Whereas the population is at present distributed almost equally between the country and the town, and ten cities have over one hundred thousand inhabitants, with the trend continuing at the same level it is estimated that by 1980 the urban population will be almost double that of the rural areas (Posada, 1962).

All Latin American countries show the same movement from the countryside to the towns and a phenomenal growth of urban concentrations. Over half the population of Mexico, Uruguay and

Ecuador live in towns, while in Argentina and Chile the proportion approaches two-thirds. All the state capitals have a disproportionately large part of the urban population: Buenos Aires has almost four million people, while the next city of Argentina, Rosario, has 620,000; Caracas has quadrupled its population since 1940, and has one and a half million of Venezuela's total population of eight and a half millions. The loss of people is exacerbated for the countryside by the fact that those who leave are generally the most intelligent and educated, above the average for the rural areas and indeed for the cities (Reyes Carmona, 1965). At the same time the increase of population also strains the city's resources, almost to breaking point in places such as São Paulo. The urban areas have in the past been better provided with schools than the country, but the sudden rise in numbers is outstripping present facilities. The young people who constitute a growing proportion of the urban population are clamouring for more than places in educational institutions. The aspirations of the student generation are becoming a significant factor in the debate about social reform.

Nor is the loss of population the only way in which the rural areas suffer to the benefit of the town. The growth of industry, which is linked with the increase of urban population, depends largely on raw materials imported from abroad by means of the foreign exchange earnings of the agricultural products. Some critics argue that urban industrialization is taking place at the direct cost of rural development. Whatever the truth of the assertion, steel and concrete are encroaching on the country and burying the past. Provincial towns all over Latin America, which up to a few years ago preserved in their architecture much of the imperial era, are now rapidly transforming themselves, tearing down the relics of the past. Everywhere the old style is disappearing, colonial dwellings with whitewashed walls and low red-tiled roofs are being ripped out, and in their place are shooting upward office blocks and sophisticated apartments twenty or thirty storeys high. Factories are spilling an industrial population over the surrounding countryside. The air is rarely still from the whine of aeroplanes. With the spread of technology comes the need for a form of education different from the traditional, which will equip the rising generations with the professional knowledge of the engineer and, even more urgently in demand, the skills of the technician and craftsman.

The ancient baroque churches stand as a reminder that the old order is not entirely dead and that the priest and the leading families of the past even now hold some sway. There is, indeed, in the cities still a wide disparity between the educational opportunities open to the privileged and those open to the poor – among whom are usually counted the Indian, the mestizo and the mulatto – particularly at the higher and secondary levels. This is in part because tradition persists in the modern city. The secondary school has for long in Latin America been almost solely a channel to the university and positions of leadership. Such aspirations could only be entertained by the children of the élite, and were beyond the vision of the masses. There is also the matter of payment. The majority of secondary schools are private and depend on the pupils' fees to pay their way, and even the state schools are not free. Secondary education is virtually restricted to the wealthier classes, though some parents of modest means make heroic sacrifices to provide education for their children. Some even starve themselves in order to let their children have this advantage.

Even more marked, however, is the difference between the provision of schools in the towns and in the country. Only the cities, and particularly the capitals, provide anything like enough places in the primary schools, though in the face of rapidly increasing numbers complete provision has proved impossible. In the rural areas, over the whole continent, less than half the eligible children attend primary school, and in the remote areas enrolment falls far short of the average (Debeauvais, 1967). For work on the land, until modern methods begin to demand new skills, formal schooling has not been essential. In some countries, such as Honduras and the Dominican Republic, the duration of the primary course as laid down by law has been less in the country than in the town, and even in those countries where the discrepancies have been legally eliminated, as in Colombia and Brazil recently, rural children spend a comparatively brief period in school, even in the face of regulations. If the children start late and drop out early, barely attaining literacy, the fault lies in the poverty and ignorance of the parents, the lack of medical care and malnutrition, and in the long distances to be travelled. The poorer amenities of the country attract less than a just proportion of the teaching force and more than a fair share of the unqualified (Debeauvais, 1967). In contrast, the developing modern economy of the town provides both the incentive and resources to place a basic education within the reach of greater numbers.

The past has contributed to the disparity of educational opportunity between social classes, between racial groups and between town- and country-dwellers. There are, however, factors which make for cohesion. Though there are many indigenous languages spoken, except in the comparatively small Guyanas, Spanish and Portuguese, have for centuries been the languages of administration and education. The Roman penal code and the Catholic faith are accepted almost everywhere. Urbanization and the development of communications are leading to a greater uniformity of outlook, and even the eruption of violence has played a positive role in underlining the urgency of the need to eradicate gross social and economic inequalities.

Education itself is an acknowledged factor in the emergence of wider loyalties, and in the overall development of the region.

Easier communication has also brought Latin America closer to the outside world and the possibilities of overseas aid for educational development, with its promise of expert advice and rapid growth, yet equally with the danger of divided counsel and divided motivation.

2

The legal basis, policy and finance

Conscious of the cultural disparity existing in their countries Latin American constitution-makers and politicians since Independence have placed great store on education as the mould of the nation. The Constitution of Peru lays down that primary education will be free and obligatory, and will take its inspiration from the enhancement – *engrandecimiento* – of the nation and human solidarity. The Chilean Constitution of 1925 uses more general terms, speaking of the child comprehending the highest civic and social ideals. Article 166 of the Brazilian Constitution refers to education based on the principles of liberty and human solidarity as the right of every child. The constitution drawn up after the Mexican revolution of 1917 required schools to instil in their pupils a love of the mother-country together with an understanding of national problems, and to teach Spanish universally in order to bring the indigenous peoples within the family of the nation. Implementing constitutional provisions, from 1934 onwards, the Argentine Government formed a series of joint commissions with a view to eliminating divergences in primary school courses in the interests of national cohesion. Everywhere cultural differences were to be harmonized under the orderly wand of the schoolmaster.

In most countries freedom of conscience is constitutionally guaranteed and any religious or private organization may legally set up school. In practice, the Roman Catholic Church benefits particularly in those countries which would claim that the Catholic faith is a vital element of national life. Peru is typical in giving the Roman Church constitutional protection in its educational work, and a monopoly of religious instruction in public schools. In Colombia a Concordat with the Vatican in 1887 confirmed the terms of the Constitution signed the year before which provided for the Church to be associated with the administration of the educational system. During periods of Liberal Party dominance the agreement was the target for turbulent criticism, and during the Presidency of Alfonso Lopez between 1934 and 1938 the Church lost control of education. However, in 1942 a new Concordat restored its privileges. The Church accepted the specific obligation to provide primary schools in the remote eastern *llanos* until the development of the territory and the growth of population justified setting up a civil authority capable of taking over the provision of education. Similarly, although there is no precise agreement, the Colombian State has long relied on religious organizations for the running of secondary schools.

From time to time the role of the Church has not escaped criticism. The Mexican Constitution of 1917 allowed the establishment of private schools, provided the permission of the State was obtained, and the schools run in conformity with the principles set out in the Constitution and the programme of the state schools. However, religious influence was specifically restrained. Religious bodies, ministers or any society closely connected with the propagation of any particular creed were not permitted to engage upon any activities concerned with primary, secondary or normal education, or the education of workers, though in practice this limitation is now observed only in the primary sector. In 1945 El Salvador similarly moved from a somewhat anti-clerical position when it annulled the constitutional provision that teaching in government schools should be wholly secular. These instances are indications of underlying antagonism which nevertheless has not generally been sufficiently strong to threaten the privileges lawfully enjoyed by the Church in several Latin American countries. Guyana, outside the Latin sphere, offers a sharp contrast. It has not, for the sake of a common culture, attempted to place any restriction on the right of religious bodies to provide education. No single religious denomination enjoys special legal privileges and in consequence schools are set up by every conceivable Christian sect, and recently also by Islamic and Buddhist communities.

The administration of education

Where creating national consciousness is in the forefront of educational aims, the administration of schools, as might be expected, is centralized in the hands of the State. Article 41 of the revised Colombian Constitution of 1945, after emphasizing that liberty of teaching is guaranteed, nevertheless goes on to say that the State shall exercise the right of general inspection and care over all institutions of learning, public or private, in order to ensure the fulfilment of the social purposes of culture and the best intellectual, moral and physical development of the students. In general in the unitary states, control of education, including such matters as regulating the school year, determining curricula, setting examinations and laying down scales for teachers' salaries, and in Peru the appointment of teachers, is vested in the national Ministry of Education. The Colombian Ministry, for example, has a Technical Branch with six divisions corresponding to the various types of educational programme, and an Administrative Branch which is concerned with recruitment, teachers' conditions, with budgets and general services. The Minister is advised by a National Education Council which brings him in contact with the thinking of the world of education as well as of other sectors of national life, and helps him to take a comprehensive view of the problems of education.

In spite of his very considerable powers, however, the Minister is not always in a position to effect changes and improvements. Though a unitary state, Colombia has a measure of administrative decentralization. The Minister appoints Directors of Education, but he has to work through local authorities which have certain responsibilities for primary education. The trend has been to delegate more responsibility to these authorities in such relatively minor matters as the provision of nursery schools and selection for national scholarships, though in 1961 the Ministry took back from local control the responsibility for the salaries of primary teachers as the burden had become too great for any but the central government to carry. The National Congress normally has the opportunity to accept or reject any legislation concerning education which the Minister might present to it. The Minister, however, is entitled to issue decrees, with the sanction of the Cabinet, and in recent years has effected significant reforms by this procedure. For example, Decree NO. 45 of 1962 amended the curricula of secondary schools to bring them in line with the resolutions of the Inter-American Conference on Secondary Education which was held in Santiago de Chile in 1954–5.

In the federal states, Brazil, Mexico and Venezuela, though there is some centralization, the provinces have even greater responsibilities. The Brazilian Education Law of 1962, *Lei de Diretrizes Basses da Educacão*, aimed at decentralization of the educational system to meet the needs of what is rather a continent than a single country. French influence had been paramount and the new law represented a compromise between the former tradition and North American trends, allowing more liberty to the states in the primary and middle sectors. It set up a Federal Council of Education as the educational policy-making body for the whole of Brazil, with members chosen for their knowledge and experience of educational matters, who would give their duties 'priority over any others which they may have elsewhere'. The Council's responsibilities included taking measures to improve educational research at all levels, to establish curricula in five compulsory subjects of the secondary course – Portuguese, mathematics, general science, history and geography – and the authorization of the statutes and curricula of new federal and private universities. The executive body charged with the implementation of these functions was the Ministry of Education.

At the same time – and this was an innovation – State Educational Councils were created to adapt the system of primary and secondary schools to the needs of the states, some of which are urbanized and some almost entirely rural. São Paulo remained the only state with responsibility for higher education, which elsewhere was a federal matter. Secondary and primary education, however, were state responsibilities, except for the federal schools such as 'Pedro Segundo' in Rio de Janeiro, and the Ginasios-Colegios de Aplicão attached to university faculties of Philosophy, Science and Letters to facilitate teaching practice for trainee middle school teachers, who were a federal responsibility. Even though the staffs of the training schools belonged to the universities, the syllabus was the same as that laid down for other secondary schools.

The State Education Council, working through its Secretariat, controlled the Inspectorate, laid down the curricula for the three optional subjects in consultation with the secondary schools, and took charge generally of the administration of the school systems. The Law encouraged freedom and variety in the optional subjects in order to allow the states to adapt the syllabus to the particular needs of the area. The choice was open to reject the traditional disciplines in preference to vocational subjects when this was appropriate. The duration of the courses, however, conformed to the criteria set down by the Federal Council. Although the choice of textbooks was left to individual schools, the Secretariat exercised considerable influence. The states were also responsible for the training of primary school teachers. The Councils devolved some of their responsibility for primary education on to industrial, commercial and agricultural enterprises employing more than one hundred persons, which were required by law to provide free schools.

The Constitution of Mexico also provides the legal framework for state and municipal as well as federal education. At the federal level there is a Secretariat headed by a Secretary for Education of cabinet status who is responsible for the financing of buildings, national educational campaigns such as the literacy campaign of 1946, textbooks and the appointment of teachers in the federal district. Generally speaking he shares his responsibilities with the state and municipal authorities who are primarily responsible for the provision of schools and other institutions of learning. Teachers' terms of service and salaries are fixed at the federal level by a 'Comisión Nacional de Escalafón' on which the Teachers' Union has representation. Each authority, however, appoints its own teaching staffs.

It is not only the provincial authorities which have to be gratified by the Ministry of Education, even in the highly centralized countries. At the middle level of education the Colombian Minister, like many of his Latin American colleagues, depends greatly on the effort of private bodies, the most important being the Catholic Church which, as has been noted, takes on the burden of providing primary education in the remote areas. It is true that independent schools are subject to the overall control of the Ministry, yet not much progress has been made towards co-ordinating the development of the private with the public sector at this level, less indeed than is attained at the higher level through the Association of Colombian Universities. Some schools fall within the portfolios of other ministries. The Ministry of Agriculture has a considerable adult programme through its Extension Division, just as in Bolivia the Ministry of Rural Affairs controls some rural schools. The Ministry of Home Affairs, through its Community Development Division, organizes literacy classes and training programmes in connection with village development, and has an Indigenous Affairs Division with similar educational functions as the Mexican Office of Indian Affairs.

Apart from these overt educational links between the various ministries, the whole of the Government's development programmes clearly rests on an educational base. What is involved is not simply the training of technical personnel in the numbers required by the various programmes but also a general raising of the educational level of the whole of the population. Since the 1958 Seminar in Washington on 'Planeamiento Integral de la Educación' planners have been aware of this, yet even so the Colombian Ministry of Education is not alone in feeling that it has not hitherto achieved the required measure of co-ordination with the central government's organs of national planning, though the machinery does exist for co-operation with the Administrative Planning Department, the National Statistics Office and the Budget Office of the Treasury. At the same time the offers of the international organizations, of which the Alliance for Progress is the most affluent provider, have to be fitted into the national jigsaw without discouraging their generous inclinations, and this has not proved a task free of ruffled pride in spite of the Office for Joint Educational Programmes created in the Ministry to harmonize various schemes of aid from overseas.

The malaise which goes with the difficulty in co-ordinating plans amounts to a more deep-seated disease in not a few Ministries of Education. Too often the resources in material and in professional personnel are inadequate for the tasks in hand. The inspectorates are not large enough, nor the staffs sufficiently experienced to exercise decisive influence. Lacking understanding of the broad issues involved, and sometimes motivated by personal susceptibilities and jealousies, officers have preferred feeble half measures. In some states the senior posts are generally political appointments, the incumbents changing with a change of government. The custom, no doubt, should ensure a loyal effort to implement the policies of the government in power, though this has not been the experience recently of Colombia, where the peculiar circumstances arising out of the agreement between the two traditional parties, the Conservatives and the Liberals, make it difficult for any policy to be pursued with vigour. The National Front agreement, as it was called, provided for a fifty-fifty sharing of public service appointments of this kind, and consequently during the decade it has been in force decisions have been difficult to reach in the Ministry of Education, as in the other ministries.

Educational reform

In short, the government institutions have not proved delicately adjusted machines capable of achieving fully the purposes expressed in so many constitutions. Nevertheless, the realization that something must be done about the disparity of educational opportunity has struck home, and where the idealist has not managed to follow through his claims for universal social justice, the demographer has brandished the dire warning of the census figures. The turning-point in the development of education in Latin America may turn out to be 1956, when the Organization of American States co-operated with Unesco in arranging a conference on Free and Compulsory Education. After the Conference ended in Lima, the Ministers of Education held their second periodic meeting, when they recognized the sterility of educational systems working in isolation from the trends of the economy, and recommended the adoption of planning methods which would assert the importance of linking the economic, social, cultural and educational sectors in any overall process of development. In the subsequent years a number of conferences on education and planning were held, and in 1961 the Alliance for Progress in its ten-year plan set out the goals to be attained to make education a serviceable instrument of progress. In 1962 the Conference on Education and Economic and Social Development issued the 'Declaration of Santiago de Chile', where the meetings were held. This document constituted a charter, so to speak, for future action. It set ambitious objectives, including universal primary education by 1970, and by the same date a threefold increase in secondary school enrolment and a doubling of the numbers in higher education. It was agreed that not less than 15 per cent of the funds provided under the Alliance for Progress should be devoted to education, and 4 per cent of the Gross National Product. At the same time it was accepted that there should be the closest co-ordination between educational development and social and economic planning. In order to achieve this, each country would undertake surveys of trained manpower needs and would look into means of improving the efficiency of the administration of education, and in particular would create administrative organs in the Ministry of Education to facilitate co-ordination with the planning of other ministries.

In addition to laying down main lines of policy the 'Declaration of Santiago' recorded detailed proposals for every aspect of education. It placed particular emphasis on ways of improving technical and agricultural training, and the education of adults. Proposals were made for eliminating illiteracy, including a suggestion that illiterates should have classes of general education during their period of military training. The greatest importance was accorded to primary education, which, it was generally agreed, should head budgetary priorities. Teacher training should be considered vital, but school feeding, medical and clothing services should not be neglected, and there should be adequate provision for textbooks and materials, and also for transport to bring children to school in rural areas. There were recommendations concerning the optimum size of class, and about the length of the school day and the school year. Curricula and methods should be adapted to give pupils an education which would make the most effective contribution to the development of the community, as well as being suited to their age and abilities, and teacher-training methods should equally be modified to the same ends. The recommendation concerning secondary education reiterated the conclusions reached in 1956 at Santiago, laying perhaps more stress on the need for secondary education to make a fuller contribution to economic development. The 'Declaration' recognized that secondary school teachers should receive remuneration 'equivalent to that of civil servants and others with similar academic qualifications and experience'. Universities were also urged to create conditions which would attract dedicated full-time teachers, and also to encourage in students full and responsible student participation in university affairs. Universities were particularly exhorted to improve the provision of scientists and technologists, to improve extension services to different sectors of the population, and to co-operate in national economic planning.

The Declaration was indeed a kind of manifesto whose main

themes were the allocation of the maximum resources to education and the integration of educational programmes into the national development plans. Debeauvais has pointed out that an annual increase of 16·4 per cent in expenditure would be needed to reach the targets set, or three times as much as the rate of increase of national incomes as forecast by the Alliance for Progress. And indeed when the Ministers of Education met in Bogotá in 1963 for their third Inter-American Conference they accepted the 'Declaration' as a basis for their future policies, but after reviewing progress, postponed from 1970 to 1975 the date by which the main plans, including the attainment of universal primary education, were to be completed. At this meeting, the tasks were to elaborate detailed programmes for implementing the 'Declaration' and the ten-year plan of the Alliance, to indicate priorities, and to recommend more effective methods for reaching the objectives. Three zones of priority were suggested: the training of personnel for educational administration and teaching; the integration of educational planning with national development plans, together with the modernization of educational administration and research into educational needs; and finally, the expansion of the secondary system, the development of the rural primary school and the provision of community and adult education. The Conference accepted fully the message of the author of the Alliance for Progress, which stressed the supreme importance of education in plans for economic and social development.

Colombia, hardly yet at the end of years of carnage, followed other countries in seizing on the idea of educational planning with optimism tempered with anxiety. There was an emergency plan; there were long-term intentions. In formulating its short-term plans the Ministry of Education set itself three main general objectives: to raise the cultural level of the populations; to eliminate illiteracy; and to reduce the number of children abandoning school without completing their course (Gomez Valderrama, 1964). This order of priorities indicated that the Government placed the greatest importance on the extension of provision and the improvement of the standards of primary education, and particularly in rural schools which were to be brought up to the same standard as the urban schools. The Colombian Ministry of Education, no doubt as other national education authorities facing their own unique social pattern, modified the priorities posited at Santiago and confirmed at Bogotá, in order to meet the peculiar problems bequeathed by the *violencia*. Its first plans did appear to neglect secondary and adult education, and to give insufficient support to the training of teachers and administrators. For the moment the burden of reform in these fields is being carried in a large measure by private and semi-official institutions. However, growing appreciation of the evidence provided by various studies of the educational needs of the country carried out by the Association of Universities, the Colombian Institute for Specialist Training Overseas, and the Office of Planning, Co-ordination and Evaluation of the Ministry itself suggests that the long-term plans will involve greatly increased expenditure in these fields.

Financial planning

Financial planning is the keystone of the whole edifice. The budget of every country reveals the extent of the effort to relate the ideals, so impatiently accepted at international conferences, to national environments not yet free from the backwardness of the past. The financing of education is shared in varying proportions between the central governments and the provinces and municipalities of the Latin American republics. The total expenditure has shown a steady increase since the Santiago Conference of 1956 and particularly since the launching of the Alliance for Progress in 1961. In Colombia in less than ten years the national expenditure on education multiplied more than five times. In 1963 the total funds provided by the central government, the departments and municipalities amounted to nearly 1,000 million pesos as compared with about half that sum in 1960, and less than 200 million pesos in 1955. Even before the second Inter-American Conference it was not unusual for governments to allocate a specific percentage of the national budget to ensure the growth of education. The 1946 Brazilian Constitution, for example, maintained the previous requirements whereby the federal government had to earmark 10 per cent of taxes for education, and the states and municipalities 20 per cent. In 1957 the Colombian Government fixed at 10 per cent the proportion of the national budget to be allocated to education and in 1963; after the third Conference of Ministers of Education, this figure was raised to 15·5 per cent, and again in 1966 to 20 per cent. Nevertheless, in 1962 this represented an annual expenditure per head on education of only $2·8 (US), a low figure when compared with $52·1 in the U.S.A. and $8·1 in Venezuela (Gomey Valderrama, 1964).

The Colombian statistics are analogous to those of several other countries between 1960 and 1965, when the rate of increase of public expenditure on education was steep, reaching 20 per cent per year in Peru and Ecuador, and from 7·1 to 11 per cent in most others (Debeauvais, 1967). In the previous five years six countries had increases of over 10 per cent per year, which meant a doubling of expenditure in just over seven years, and a fourfold increase in about thirteen years. Over the same period education has managed to go on increasing its relative share of the gross national product almost everywhere at the expense of other services. The 1962 conference on education and economic development called upon all states to devote 4 per cent of the GNP to education by 1965. In 1961 education had accounted for about 3 per cent of the GNP on an average throughout the continent, as compared with 2·3 per cent in 1960. Between 1957 and 1960 Venezuela increased the percentage of the GNP devoted to education from 0·85 to 2·25 per cent, a phenomenal rise, and by 1963 the proportion had reached 3·7 per cent. In Costa Rica and Panama public expenditure on education represents 34 per cent of the national budget, though it has to be allowed that these countries do not maintain armed forces. The exceptional increases which were called for by the Santiago Conference could only be maintained for a limited period of time, and it seems that the process of levelling-off may already have begun in some countries, including Costa Rica, Panama, and also Peru and Venezuela. The targets set at Santiago have already proved more difficult to attain than anticipated and the postponement of target dates from 1970 to 1975 may not be sufficient grace for some countries. The capital expenditure envisaged has risen steeply as a result of inflation, and of the increased cost of importing materials when the exchange rates moved unfavourably with the decline in the price of primary products. The experience of Ecuador in 1960 and of Peru in 1965 when teachers' salaries rose by one-third would suggest that the cost per pupil is pushed upwards as teachers keep in step with the general rise of incomes per head. The larger republics,

Brazil, Mexico and Argentina, however, are far from devoting to education a fraction of income comparable to Peru or Venezuela, or the advanced countries of the world.

Within the national figures for Colombia the expenditure on education of the departments rose over the same period roughly by the same percentage as that of the central government, and that of the municipalities less so, but still impressively. There has been, however, a tendency for the proportion of the whole contributed by both the departments and the municipalities to fall, while the proportion contributed by the central government has risen, though the relative movement has not been regular. In 1955 the central government was contributing 40·4 per cent of the total educational expenditure, as against 47·3 per cent by the departments and 12·3 per cent by municipalities. By 1963 the percentages were 46·2 per cent by the Government, 45·1 per cent by departments and 8·7 per cent from municipal sources. Since 1961 the expenditure of the Ministry of Education has surpassed that of the departments, and in 1962 indeed was 53 per cent of the whole, more than the total of the departmental and municipal contributions together. (Velez, 1964). The immediate reason for this was the legal obligation placed on the Ministry to pay the salaries of primary school teachers, formerly paid by the departments, but the trend reflects the inevitability of a changed pattern when expenditure rises steeply. Only the central government has the means of raising through national taxation and external aid the enormous sums called for by the rapid growth of the educational system. Clearly the expansion of rural primary education would not be feasible, because of lack of resources, without national and external financial support. Whether it is intended or not, elsewhere as in Colombia, national plans for the expansion of education bring the need for more funds than can normally be produced locally and sometimes a greater degree of centralized bureaucratic control.

Priorities

The belief generally accepted in recent years that Latin American countries have starved secondary education of funds in order to expand the primary sector rapidly, has been questioned on the grounds that in fact expenditure on the middle and higher sectors has been growing faster (Debeauvais, 1967). In evaluating this view it has to be realized that in those countries whose public secondary school system was in the first place poorly developed a comparatively small additional expenditure represents a high rate of increase. In any case, as far as public expenditure is concerned several countries follow Colombia in giving the primary school pride of place in the order of financial priorities. During the period 1955–63, in the programme of capital expenditure in education of the central government 60 per cent went to the primary sector, and to this may be added a further 10 per cent devoted to construction in connection with the training of primary teachers. The proportion invested in secondary education was 25 per cent, and 5 per cent in higher education (Velez, 1964). In 1960 the primary school took 15·61 per cent of the combined capital and recurrent budget of the Ministry of Education, a figure which rose to 38·13 per cent in 1963. If the budgetary figures of the departments and municipalities are added to those of the central government over 56 per cent of the total estimates for education was allocated to the primary sector in 1962 (Posada, 1962).

Including Colombia, twelve out of nineteen Latin American republics spent over half the total public expenditure on education on the primary sector in the years up to 1960, and in the case of Bolivia, Costa Rica, Nicaragua and Mexico the proportion was over 65 per cent. It is true that Colombia was one of the countries allotting the smallest part of the national education budget to the secondary level, but only Argentina, Brazil, Chile and Haiti were expanding as much as 30 per cent of the education budget at this level (Bardeci and Escondrillas, 1963).

The relative figures would be considerably modified if the expenditure by private bodies on secondary education could be included. In countries where private schools are more numerous than state schools at the second level, the financial contribution from independent sources sometimes surpasses that of the State. Moreover, subsidies to private institutions for buildings and salaries, such as have been provided by the Brazilian National Fund for Secondary Education, are uncommon, and Colombia is not unique in providing virtually no subsidy at all. Consequently, public expenditure does not necessarily represent the total contribution of a community to this sector and the official figures do not reveal all that is spent on it. In any case, though the proportions of the central government's education budget devoted to secondary and higher education may have shown a tendency to fall in some countries in the face of steeply rising expenditure on primary schools, the absolute amounts have risen appreciably. The Colombian state's contribution to universities rose from 48 million pesos in 1960 to 89 million pesos in 1963 and to secondary schools from 31 million to 55 million pesos. What does seem true, however, is that the traditional Colombian reverence for the high qualification may still be influencial in giving to universities a comparatively good deal, and this is true also of Argentina, Costa Rica, Ecuador, Paraguay and Venezuela, all of which devote an even higher proportion of the available resources to higher education.

To return to the financing of education as a whole, all the republics of Latin America except the Dominican Republic and Panama increased the proportion of the GNP devoted to education between 1957 and 1960, the years following immediately on the Santiago Conference. However, it was ominous that during the same period the benefit of increased provision was cancelled out in some countries by demographic growth and by increased costs. Colombia, Chile and Mexico were among those countries in which expenditure per head of schoolchild increased at a greater rate than the proportion of the GNP absorbed by education, whereas in Brazil, Argentina and Peru it was the other way round, or in other words, increased educational expenditure was taken up largely by the rising tide of population without necessarily any improvement in the general position.

Since economic crystal-gazing is notoriously vulnerable to unforeseen accidents, it is perhaps permissible to speculate whether events will indeed bear out the forecasts and show that Argentina, Uruguay, Brazil, Peru and Venezuela have public resources available for education sufficient to meet the ambitious targets set for 1975. However, it does already seem clear that all other South American countries will not be able to fulfil the commitments undertaken for public education without external aid, and in the private sector all except Argentina are poorly placed to meet demands from internal resources alone.

3

The primary school

One hot afternoon in 1966 on the outskirts of the village of Sasaima, some two hours' drive out of Bogotá towards the Magdelena valley, the schoolmaster was marching his charges, boys and girls of all ages, up and down the gravel of the school yard with the strident command of a sergeant-major. There in action was a primary school whose purpose in the words of the Ministry was

> to contribute to the harmonious development of the child and the building up of his personality; to help him to appreciate the values of the culture to which he belongs and particularly to inculcate the Christian concept of life and the principles of liberty and democracy which are decisive factors in the evolution of Colombian nationhood.

There are echoes in this ministerial statement of the ideals of eighteenth-century enlightenment, and of the first enthusiasm for the spread of knowledge, when in the midst of the struggle for independence decrees founding new schools were frequent throughout Latin Amerca, and new ideas, such as the monitorial system of Joseph Lancaster, were being widely tested. But Independence did not succeed in making effectual the endeavour for improvement and even now the official exhortation is too tall an order for the most favoured urban school, and far beyond the vision of this rural teacher whose sights were set much lower. The average village schoolmaster, who may have enjoyed little more than five years' primary schooling himself, whose outlook reflects the views of sterile local cliques (Wolfe, 1965), and whose methods of discipline were derived rather from a brief spell as a conscript than from the training college, could have no concept of such high-sounding ideals. Though he might set out with zeal, the discouraging circumstances of his task must dull his enthusiasm. Not that the Colombian primary teacher was any worse placed than his counterparts elsewhere on the continent, and indeed with no more than thirty-six pupils, as the Ministry claimed, the size of his class was not exceptional but roughly average (Unesco, 1963). Others were less well placed. His Mexican colleagues were likely to have fifty-four children in the first grade and only seven fewer in the other classes. No teacher without knowledge and training could avoid falling into a military approach to discipline with a class containing an age range from seven to eleven years and something around forty or even more children. In the majority of South American republics children are required to attend school for six years from the age of six, or in some countries seven. In Argentina, exceptionally, the primary school course covers seven grades. In Chile, Honduras and Colombia, the rural primary course has been shorter than the urban course, until recently in Colombia only four years, and even as little as two in some parts of the country.

Universal enrolment

In practice, the requirements of the law count for little. The average South American child in fact enjoys just over two years' primary school, as against seven in Japan and nine in the U.S.A. Over the whole continent for several decades enrolment has clearly been rising, and in 1964 Unesco reported that since 1955 it had grown by nine million from 55 to 70 per cent of the age group. The figures for Colombia started a little short of the continental average: in 1955 there were over one million at school, or 66 per cent of the age group, and over half a million absentees. By 1960 the position had improved with 1,297,400 primary school pupils out of an age group of 1,844,182, representing 70·4 per cent. In the five years following 1958 primary enrolment in Mexico rose by nearly one and a half millions. The figures represent a tremendous effort and real improvement of the position. At the same time the achievement has been accompanied by some straining of resources, which has postponed the eradication of serious shortcomings of the primary system. The very size of the increase may divert attention from the simple truth that quality may have suffered in the process of expansion, and even the enrolment statistics themselves can be misleading. When the first primary class contains children not only of the normal statutory starting age of, say, seven, but also older, it is clear that the number of children enrolled may exceed the total number of seven-year-olds. Moreover, where children outside the seven to twelve age range, which is normal for courses of six years duration, are at school, it is possible to have total enrolments higher than the total of the age range. It has been suggested that most countries are precisely in that position, with enrolment ratios of more than 100 per cent, and that only four countries, Bolivia, Guatemala, Haiti and Nicaragua in 1965 had ratios below 85 per cent (Debeauvais, 1966, p. 364). Such calculations, however, give a false picture and hide the fact that there are considerable numbers of school age who should be enrolled but who are not. Though the position may not be entirely clear the general view that there are many children who do not go to school at all in some countries is probably not mistaken; the assumption that the enrolment problem is solved or well on the way to a satisfactory outcome is too optimistic.

Enrolment is not, of course, the end of the problem. No less serious is the extent of irregular attendance and wastage, or dropout. The extreme poverty and ignorance of the parents, malnutrition and lack of medical care, and the long distances to be travelled, are common causes for spasmodic attendance.

The children give up school altogether for the same reasons, and also because of the need for the child's labour on the farm or to supplement the family budget. Though there has been some recent improvement, Unesco calculated in 1960 that of every thousand children who entered primary school in Latin America 866 left before reaching the sixth grade, and half left after one year. It has been estimated that more than a third of the pupils of Latin American primary schools are in their first grade, the rest being spread progressively more thinly over the remaining five or six grades. The inefficiency resulting from the wastage is not remedied by the practice of requiring pupils to repeat a year of the course if they appear backward. In Argentina only 21 per cent of the pupils who start primary school finish their school career in the normal period.

To rid the primary system of these disabilities is not merely a question of persuading parents to send their children to school regularly, and of finding ways of saving pupils from repeating a year's work. Involved are a number of complicating problems. While it is demonstrable that without wastage the average cost per pupil would be reduced by 70 per cent, the cost of catering for the additional numbers would raise the expenditure on primary education by about a quarter. The first need would be for more and better-qualified teachers who would not so lack inspiration as to drive bored and disappointed scholars from the classroom. A large amount of new construction would be necessary, especially in those countries where the shortage of space already deprives many classes of a full day's teaching because a two-shift system has to be practised. Until these deficencies can be made good, many children will continue to reach the end of their school career with literacy barely attained, or at least barely firmly established, and the goal of cultural homogeneity will remain no more than a fantasy.

In respect of enrolment and wastage Guyana has had some advantage, though not great, over neighbouring Venezuela, whose record is, however, somewhat better than the Latin American average. Of the six to twelve age group 85 per cent were enrolled as compared with 81 per cent in Venezuela in 1965. Eight years' schooling is compulsory, and 75 per cent of the twelve to fourteen age group were also attending school, though of course some were in secondary schools. There was overcrowding, just as in the neighbouring Latin countries. In fact, over half the primary schools had insufficient space and a few employed the double-shift system. The Guyana Development Plan for 1966–72 envisaged some quantitative growth of the primary system in order to meet increases in the school-age population. It did not, however, make provision for the attainment of universal primary education within the period, but sought simply to keep the proportion of the age group enrolled at 85 per cent, on the grounds that with limited resources available it was better to concentrate on improving the quality of education than to seek goals which are possibly more associated with prestige than the real needs of the present. This is an attitude which comes more easily to a country with a literacy rate of 83 per cent than to those in which illiteracy is a serious obstacle to national development. The Latin American countries have not felt able to take the more philosophical point of view but have persisted in setting their sights hopefully on having every child at the school desk if not by 1970, then by 1975.

School building

Guyana, like its continental neighbours, faces a huge school construction problem to replace condemned buildings, to eliminate overcrowding and to meet the needs of an estimated 20 per cent rise in the school population by 1972, without considering universal provision. The Development Plan speaks of forty-six thousand new places to meet these demands. Since buildings are a heavy drain on resources the Guyana Government has made a reappraisal of the standards of construction previously thought essential, and has emphasized the need for economy and simplicity in school design. Appreciable savings have been achieved in the cost of labour by the use of self-help methods, and six thousand school places have been constructed under a scheme carried out in conjunction with the World Food Programme, whereby food aid is provided to the participants in the projects in proportion to the work performed (Guyana Government, 1966). Ecuador, benefiting from the assistance of the 'Cooperative for American Relief Everywhere', better known as CARE, in a like manner made local contributions in land, materials and labour, amounting to almost half the cost, towards building some three hundred classrooms a year. Mexico has an even more formidable task than Guyana. Faced with 1·7 million children of school age not at school in 1959, and the prospect of the school population rising by over one million to 7·2 millions by 1970, the Government launched an eleven-year national plan for improving and expanding primary education. The Plan foresaw the construction of 27,440 classrooms, the greater part in the rural areas, as well as the provision of over eighteen thousand homes for rural teachers. Such building led to a steep rise in expenditure, and in 1963 the primary budget had reached $2,311 (US), of which the Federal Government contributed $1,449, more than twice the total five years previously (C. Cano, 1964). Very good progress towards these targets has been achieved. By 1963 over twenty-two thousand new classrooms had been constructed, the majority for primary schools.

Assuming an average of forty pupils to each classroom, Colombia's existing deficiencies in 1963 were 22,463 class units, though some estimates put the figure as high as 29,202, without taking into consideration replacement of dilapidated buildings. A further twelve to eighteen thousand classrooms were estimated to be required to meet the needs of the increasing number of children of primary age, bringing the total to between thirty-five and fifty thousand. A four-year building plan was drawn up which aimed to produce 2,800 classrooms a year. It was indeed hoped that the rate could be raised to three thousand a year and that the major part of the deficit could be wiped out by 1972 or 1973. It was anticipated that the building would be financed from internal sources supported by external aid.

These hopes have already been dashed. Almost as soon as the plan was formulated the terms of trade turned against Colombia and the economic and financial crisis which followed severely reduced the possibilities for public investment. The failure of external aid offered under the Alliance for Progress to reach the expected level during this period intensified the difficulties, as did also the increase in cost of imported materials as a result of the devaluation of the peso in 1962 and again in 1964. To make matters worse the supply of locally produced material and skilled labour fell short of expectations. In order to overcome some of the problems, and particularly to co-ordinate international and national resources, to formulate more realistic plans and to increase the administrative efficiency of the building programme, the Administrative Office for Joint Educational Programmes was set up in the Ministry of Education. There organization resulted in some improvement, without making it possible to reach the targets set. In 1963, for example, only 1,521 classrooms were completed, with a further 661 still under construction. The terms of trade have more recently shown signs of turning, but this experience of Colombia reveals the hazards of the market and the blocks caused by dearth of trained human resources which the Latin American countries encounter in their attempts to expand primary school construction plans. In 1964 the United States President could claim that the Alliance for Progress had constructed seven thousand classrooms in the previous year. Perhaps the very generous North American influence and aid, which was part of the effort, have led some Latin American countries to set their building standards too high and not to give enough attention to economical building. It is ironical in the circumstances that in order to develop her cheap school building plans in 1966 Guyana recruited a Unesco architect who was in fact Colombian.

The quality of primary education

However, as the attainment of universal enrolment loses some of its immediacy, the improvement of the quality of primary education becomes the most pressing problem, even more urgent than that of providing buildings. In almost any region of the continent the primary schools can offer examples of the same depressing picture. In Guyana, for example, the curriculum was until recently extremely out of date, including in the lower classes such fossils as simple parsing and analysis of sentences in the English syllabus, and in arithmetic complicated fractions which modern educationists believe to be beyond the ability and understanding of the majority of children of primary school age. To make things worse the brighter children were frequently segregated even at the early age of eight and crammed with English and arithmetic for the scholarship examination, which would offer a small fraction of them the chance of a free academic secondary education. Methods are still old-fashioned; untrained teachers can do no more than ape the ways of an older generation. One observer has described his impressions of going into a school at the end of a hot day and 'finding there in the dark and smelly classroom, heavy with the smell of stale perspiration, forty or fifty children with a tired teacher. And what were they doing? They were learning the definitions of nine different kinds of pronouns – personal, possessive, relative, or conjunctive, reflexive, interrogative, indefinite, demonstrative, and emphasising' (James, 1959). Similar futile sessions could be witnessed in many a primary school in the tropical Latin countries. Everywhere, including in those Ministries of Education which have put quantitative objectives at the head of their priorities, there is a full realization of the widespread poor quality of primary education, particularly in the rural areas. Nor is there anything unique in the effort of Colombia to improve it, though there the rural areas are less well provided than generally. In 1963, as part of the broader purpose of making primary education available to the whole age group of Colombian children, the reform of the primary system was decreed to bring the rural in line with the urban schools by making a primary course of five years' duration from the age of seven obligatory for both. At the same time the content of the course was revised. The teaching of

the mother tongue, almost everywhere Spanish, was to be intensified, and a groundwork of instruction in general science was to be
included in the last three years' work to make it more relevant to the
modern world. Methods of instruction were also to be changed and
adapted more closely to the child's stage of development, and to the
way of life of the area in which the school was situated.

Research and experiment

With the plans for reform went an upsurge of interest in research
into primary education. An Institute for Pedagogical Research was
established in the Colombian National Pedagogical University in
1962, and included in its tasks the analysis of teaching methods,
elaboration and evaluation of curricula, and production of school
texts and visual aids, together with the publication of the results of
its work in special bulletins and in a regular review. The major
Unesco Project which developed out of the Regional Conference of
Latin American States on Free and Compulsory Education held in
Lima in 1956, had called for research into the problems of primary
schools and invited universities to lend their assistance. The
Universities of São Paulo in Brazil and Santiago de Chile were
particularly selected for co-operation in this way, but the Pedagogical University of Bogotá was by no means unique in following their
example in investigating primary education. Increasingly throughout
the continent university education departments have paid attention
to this aspect of social research. Outside the universities too there
was a quickening of interest in research. In Brazil, for example, a
National Institute for Pedagogical Studies was established within
the Ministry of Education. The Institute worked through a federal
and five regional centres, all situated in the eastern littoral states,
and all associated with experimental schools such as the Guatemala
School attached to the centre in Rio de Janeiro. In these establishments a good deal of experimentation with programme organization,
activity projects, teaching methods and curricula, took place, together with research into such related matters as varying learning
rates and abilities, and has led to the publication of practical
material including a guide for teachers of mathematics in the first
grade and similar handbooks.

There was also experimentation and research in various training centres. As another token of the Unesco Major Project's special preoccupation with the training of teachers four model training colleges were set up at Pamploma in Colombia, Teguciagalpa in Honduras, Jinopete y San Marcos in Nicaragua and San Pablo del Lago in Ecuador. The Instituto Superior de Educación Rural at Pamplona, like its sister institutes, specialized in courses in co-operation, community development and agricultural techniques, but it also directed its attentions towards improving the rural primary school. It had annexed to it a special primary school which served as a laboratory for investigating and testing methods which could be used in the village schools, and especially in those operating with only a single master. In the meantime a number of studies of primary and rural education were published. In the year following the Lima meetings, M. B. Lourenço Filho contributed a monograph on the 'Primary School Curricula in Latin America' to the Unesco series of *Studies and Documents*. From 1956 the Organization of American States began publication of its review *La Educación*, which gave continued prominence to discussion of progress in the primary school from issue NO. 9, devoted to rural education to issue NO. 33 in 1964, which concentrated on the primary school.

Dissemination of information joined research and experiment as inseparable companions of reform. Some of the experimentation in Latin America was carried out in the field. Colombia had been represented at the Seminar on the single-teacher school which was arranged at the Inter-American Rural Education Centre at Rubio in Venezuela in 1959, and it was not surprising that the Government responded readily to the suggestion to look further into the possibilities of this type of school made by the XIVth International Conference on Public Education organized by Unesco and the International Bureau of Education at Geneva in 1961. The idea appealed particularly to the educators of Latin America where so many of the rural schools were operating with a staff of one: in Uruguay over half the rural schools were of this type and in Colombia at the beginning of the decade over ten thousand schools had no more than one teacher (*La Educación*, NO. 24, 1962).

In 1964 the Ministry of Education in Bogotá launched a group of model single-teacher schools as a pilot project under the direct supervision of its experts, and thereafter attached a practice one-teacher school to all normal schools in order to give the trainees experience in this type of school. The purpose of the pilot schemes was to pioneer methods for all rural schools, which would indicate the means of attaining universal literacy, the solution to the problem of teacher shortage, and the path to many associated advantages, such as the end of the rural transport problem, the disappearance of the disparity between rural and urban standards, and the halting of the migration to the towns (Gomez Valderrama, 1964). Quite a burden to put on the back of one poor village teacher.

There had been earlier more broad-based experiments in connection with primary schools. Decree NO. 146 of 1956 established six pilot primary schools in Colombia with the aim of clarifying the objectives of the first stages of education, of drawing up a programme of work adapted to the development of the child, and working out practical methods for the guidance of the teacher. The Bogotá pilot school took both boys and girls, whereas the others were less typical of the usual school situation: two in Barranquilla and Pasto catered for girls only, while the remaining three at Bucaramanga, Cali and Medellin had only boys. All were reasonably well equipped and staffed, the Bogotá school with twenty-six members of staff for 878 pupils, and the others having a ratio of pupils to each member of staff ranging from twenty-five to thirty-nine. The school in the capital had a Director as well as an Assessor, while the others with the exception of Medellin had a Director without teaching commitments. These schools were working in conditions approaching the ideal and consequently the lessons learnt from them had only a limited relevance to the average school.

Rural pilot projects

Another promising Colombian scheme designed to improve the standard of rural education works through schools grouped around a nucleus – the *núcleo escolar*, which has been defined as a system of rural schools in orbit, so to speak, around a suitably located central school, which may be boarding. The central school may also offer a higher stage to children of the sectional schools who otherwise would not be able to complete the primary cycle. This nodal centre is equipped with materials and staff under a Director, who controls and co-ordinates all the activities, both school and extra-mural, of the branch schools. The Director has two distinct staffs. One is a teaching staff of well-qualified teachers who organize the central school to serve as a guide and stimulus to the branches. This team works on four fronts. It is concerned with material problems; it builds and repairs schools, installs sanitary services and water and light, it organizes school gardens and farms as well as sports facilities. Its second task is the administration both of the central school and the branches. A vital part of its role is the planning of the school work. It is responsible for drawing up programmes for all the schools in the network, and it has a duty to introduce progressive methods and projects adapted to the particular needs of the locality. It produces teaching materials for use in the whole system, and it helps to improve the professional competence of the sectional teachers by seminars, short courses and demonstration. Its last role is social. It organizes a meals service, parents' associations and community development committees, young farmer's clubs, literacy groups and so on. Side by side with this teaching body is a team of technical demonstrators whose work lies mainly with adults outside the school, and is concerned with promoting the development of the community. This team consists of an agricultural extension worker, a health and sanitation officer, a rural crafts teacher and a literacy expert.

The *núcleo escolar* is more than just a village school for children. It sets out to improve the nature and quality of rural education as part of the process of developing the whole community. It is concerned with the children in the adult community to which they belong. The starting-point of the whole programme of work is, in fact, a social, economic and cultural survey of the area carried out by the joint team. The organization and content of the programmes is related to the life of the region as it appears from this preliminary research. Significant results have been claimed for these schools, two hundred of which had been established by 1963 as a result of collaboration between the Ministries of Education, Health, Agriculture, Public Works, and several public and private bodies including the Association of Coffee Growers. The number of children passing through them rose from 3,700 in 1960 to 11,093 in 1962, while over the same period the number of adults dealt with rose from 1,500 to 12,827. The *núcleos escolares* have succeeded, it is claimed, in producing fundamental changes in the behaviour of groups who formerly lived in a state of open warfare: the former guerrilla chieftains are now the chairmen of development commit- tees and the captains of sports teams. However, though these schools offer promise they constitute only a fraction of the total number of primary schools in Colombia, and handle less than 1 per cent of the children of primary age. An eminent Ecuadorian editor has complained that Latin America seems to have difficulty in get- ting beyond the 'sample' stage, as he calls it. There are plenty of model schools, but they do not manage to convey their lessons to all schools (J. Larrea, 1963). It remains a gloomy truth that in spite of the various efforts at improvement in Colombia and elsewhere, the average primary schools both in the rural and urban areas of the less well-developed countries of the continent are unchanged. They are still capable of no more than providing the elementary essentials of instruction to make the children of the masses useful servants of society, and they often achieve less. The progressive reforms attempted by every minister of education make little headway, partly at least for the same reason that the Lancastrian schools did not prosper, in spite of the support of the Liberator in the early days of Independence, because there is not enough money to provide the buildings and materials and to staff the medical and social services which might eliminate wastage, but even more because of the shortage of adequately trained teachers.

Radio and television

A number of countries have attempted to get around the dearth of qualified teachers by the use of radio and television in the class- room. Since the Second World War Guyana has built up an efficient schools broadcasting unit with well-qualified staff, many of whom trained with the British Broadcasting Corporation. There is little to criticize in the material broadcast or in its production, and if the best use has not always been made of the lessons, the fault has been at the receiving end, in the schools where physical and technical difficulties have not made easier the task of the teacher, all too often unqualified. Sound radio has been used in Peru, Brazil, Chile and other Latin American countries to supplement the resources of the primary school.

Television, however, is now attracting the attention of educational authorities. While in Chile exchange difficulties over the import of receivers has stood in the way of regular schools' television broadcasting, in neighbouring Peru primary education has been broadcast through both government and unofficial channels. 'Televisión Popular' broadcasting from Arequipa has been particularly successful in maintaining a high standard of production with shoestring resources for both secondary schools and adult classes as well as primary schools. Mexico has been particular active with educational broadcasting. Some emanates from unofficial sources: the University of Monterrey puts out primary as well as other programmes, and the Latin American Institute for Education through the Cinema produces film material for distribution over the whole of the continent. Within the governmental organization the Department for Audio-Visual Education supplies material to both official and private networks, and the Federal Government has plans for a network of microwave transmitters which will bring an educational television service within reach of all schools in the country. Colombia, too, is one of those countries which has established a schools division in the national radio and television organization. The Schools Television Unit was started in 1963 with the help of the American Agency for International Development, which supplied studio equipment and school receivers, and of the Peace Corps, which provided technicians and producers and a team of teacher advisers to work in the schools, some seventy people in all. The main subjects televised were mathematics and science, each to almost all primary standards, though lessons in Spanish, geography and history, and music were also given to some classes. Each lesson consisted of three parts: fifteen minutes class preparation; fifteen minutes broadcast; fifteen minutes use of the material after the broadcast. Teachers were supplied with a guide which gives in printed form the material for the lesson as laid down in the programme of the Ministry, as well as guidance to the class teacher on how to organize his lesson. The teacher also had the regular help of the Peace Corps volunteers, though some of these lacked experience both of teaching and educational television. The Educatonal Television Unit organizes short courses and demonstrations from time to time to give teachers and producers the opportunity for exchanging ideas and discussing the best way of using the televised lessons. A

special programme to encourage teachers to evaluate the broadcasts is televised on Saturday mornings. In 1966 the programme
was expanded, with the help of the Ministry of Health and the
National Institute of Nutrition, to include lessons on nutrition,
health and physical education, and plans were made to introduce
literacy classes. The programmes were televised during term-time for
two and a half hours in the mornings and almost two hours in the
afternoons. They were received mostly by state schools and principally in the region around the capital, though the coverage expanded
each year. In 1966 over three hundred thousand children benefited
from the televised lessons. Educational television has not been
running long enough to allow a fair evaluation of its impact, and it is
premature to place too much weight on the criticisms which can
easily be made of its equipment and techniques. It will no doubt
make its contribution to the improvement of the primary school as
experience is accumulated and as the university departments of
education turn their attention to training in this medium. At least
one university has made a start: the Jesuit *Javeriana* in Bogotá now
offers a course for educational television producers.

Teachers

There is no evidence, however, that sound broadcasting or television
will relieve Latin America of the necessity to expand the primary
system and to improve the work of the primary school. The key to
these problems is the training of more teachers with adequate
qualifications.

   In 1960 Unesco published a study of the 'Educational situation in
Latin America'. It was estimated that in that over five million children of school age in Latin America were not at school. Assuming
that the average class contains forty pupils 130,000 teachers would be
required to provide classes for these children, and if the further
assumption is made that the school age population would increase by
one million in the following ten years the figure would be 275,000
new teachers. The Colombian situation in this respect epitomizes
the continental. In 1962 there were some forty-three thousand
registered primary school teachers. Since only 69 per cent of the
total age group of two million children were in fact at school, something in the vicinity of fifteen thousand additional teachers would

be required to make universal primary education possible, without consideration of the natural increase in population. Primary teachers are trained in Colombia, as in the other Latin American countries, in Normal Schools, which form part of the secondary rather than the higher sector of the educational system. If numbers of colleges were the sole criterion Colombia is exceptionally well endowed and should have little problem in meeting its teacher-training targets. There are three hundred and eighteen Normal Schools in the country, sixty-two for men and the rest for women. They are, however, extremely unevenly distributed, the Province of Antioquia having fifty-six, while neighbouring Atlantico has only six, with the result that some areas remain chronically short while others are unable to absorb all the new recruits. The departments of Cundinamarca and Antioquia have a high proportion of private women's colleges, while Santander depends mostly on the official departmental schools, and the undeveloped provinces such as Guajira depend almost entirely on the central government for provision. With uneven distribution and divided responsibility there are marked differences in size, some colleges having quite inadequate resources of staff and equipment to be effective. More rational geographical distribution, some institutions amalgamating with others and some smaller units disappearing, would be essential before any great increase in output could be achieved. With almost half the colleges in private hands this would be a thorny problem, especially as the State has contributed to the maintenance of less than half of them, and as state institutions are not among the most efficient. Some growth is being achieved. The number of student teachers successfully completing courses in 1961 was 2,353, an increase of 351 over the previous year, and, with unqualified recruits, the number entering the profession each year was about three thousand (Gomez Valderrama, 1964). The position was similar in other countries, according to a Unesco publication in 1963 on 'Primary Education in Latin America'. Mexico increased her yearly output of normal graduates by 114 to 4,524, and between 1958 and 1963 provided over eight thousand additional places in the training colleges. In that period the primary teaching force, including recruits other than normal school products, rose by more than half to almost one hundred and thirty-five thousand. In 1961 Venezuela raised her production of normal graduates by 339 to 2,790, and in the five-year period ending in 1964 increased her corps of primary teachers by something around thirty thousand. Over the whole continent in 1965 the number of student teachers in colleges was growing twice as fast as that of pupils in the schools and there were reported to be five hundred and seventy thousand teachers in training, or half the total number in the profession. It is, however, premature to claim that the unqualified teacher has all but disappeared. While Argentina, whose output in 1961 was already almost twenty-two thousand trained teachers, may be producing more than she can absorb, even five times her yearly needs according to one estimate, the Latin countries to the north were a long way from keeping pace, and the Guyana Training College did not anticipate producing enough qualified teachers within the foreseeable future, in spite of a threefold increase in yearly output.

The training of teachers

Finding teachers in the right numbers is only one aspect of the problem. Many of the so-called qualified teachers are deficient in basic general education and professional training for their task, and large numbers in service have no qualification at all beyond primary schooling. Only Argentina can claim to have no unqualified personnel, though Chile, Uruguay, Panama and the southern states of Brazil in 1961 had less than a fifth of the total teaching force without qualifications, and virtually none in state schools. In most other countries half or more of the teachers had no professional training, and in Bolivia, Colombia, Ecuador, Nicaragua and the Dominican Republic the proportion exceeded two-thirds. By 1965 the proportion of unqualified teachers over the whole of Latin America had dropped to 37 per cent. In Guyana only one in six primary teachers has had full training.

Provision of in-service training is fairly general, normally through an institution such as the Mexican 'Instituto Federal de Capacitación del Magisterio' or the Colombian 'Instituto Nacional de Capacitación y Perfeccionamiento'. These institutes offer courses by correspondence supplemented by vacation courses, and in Brazil, Guatemala, Venezuela, as well as in Colombia, the instruction is backed up by radio talks and bulletins. Large numbers of teachers usually register in the institutes, in Colombia the enrolment amounting to 14,624 in 1963, although frequently many of the registered are not actively studying. Although Argentina does not bear the same burden as other countries, the Ministry of Education offers teachers the opportunity to improve their professional competence through courses covering five hundred hours' study at the Felix Fernando Bernasconi Institute: registration is voluntary, but once enrolled the teacher must attend. The Argentine Teachers' Association also offers refresher courses.

The quality of teaching in schools must depend more on the standards set by the normal schools than remedial efforts of in-service courses, and all governments have included the normal school in their plans to improve the standards of the secondary stage. In Colombia the Government is attempting to bring the teacher-training schools in line with the academic secondary schools by organizing the work in two cycles, one of four years devoted to general studies, followed by a two-year course of professional training. This six-year course has been made compulsory for all candidates for teaching certificates, and it is expected that only those who have shown the intellectual ability and the psychological maturity and sense of vocation necessary for the task will proceed to the final professional studies. All over Latin America there is the same attempt to shake teacher training out of its traditional rut. The Unesco model rural normal schools in Colombia, Honduras, Nicaragua and Ecuador are setting the pace, as is also the Inter-American Rural Education Centre set up at Rubio in Venezuela by the Organization of American States for postgraduate training in administration and supervision of rural education. The institutions are hoping to make normal schools the driving force behind the transformation of the primary school by imbuing the teacher with a new professional zeal and competence. To achieve this many of the colleges will require better premises and equipment, more qualified staff, laboratories and libraries than they have at present, and there is no certainty that they will get them.

The status of teachers

One further obstacle to improving the effectiveness of the primary teacher remains to be discussed. Though it is probably crucial, it is rarely mentioned in official comment. Teaching in primary schools is an unattractive profession, not only because of the low salaries offered. Perhaps even more discouraging is the low status of the primary teacher, little more in the eyes of the arrogant than that of a domestic servant in some places. Even in Argentina, where teachers have a less lowly station, they have lost ground recently, having failed to maintain their cost-of-living increases at the level guaranteed by the law, in the face of rival claims from other sectors of the community. Guyana, which has the problem to a lesser degree, gave recognition to the importance of the teachers' role by inviting teachers to attend a conference in 1965 to plan a new curriculum, and it looks forward to easing the difficulty still further by associating primary teacher training with the newly established Institute of Education of university status. Notwithstanding the disadvantages under which primary teachers labour in Latin America, the indications are that with the expansion and improvement of teacher training a professional attitude will be increasingly in evidence.

4

The secondary stage

The secondary school is the kingpin of progress in the primary school, and indeed of the whole range of social and economic development. In some parts of the world over-expanded secondary education has posed a threat to university and professional standards and has flooded the labour market with unemployables. Secondary schools in Latin America have some way to go before they are in that position. They are still in the growth stage. Because the increase of pupils passing through the primary school has resulted in growing pressure at the next level, even in the five years preceding 1956 the rate of increase in secondary school enrolment was 3·3 per cent, rising in the subsequent five years to 7·87 per cent, and in the last five years has reached over 10 per cent. In terms of numbers these rates represented a rise in Colombia from 107,627 secondary pupils in 1957 to 178,343 five years later (Gomez Valderrama, 1964). Starting from almost the same figure Mexico doubled it in five years before 1963. In Brazil in the decade prior to 1961 numbers rose from five hundred and forty thousand to almost a million and a third, about 12 per cent of the twelve to eighteen age group (Lourenço-Filho, 1965). In the last twenty to thirty years some countries have multiplied their secondary school intake several times over, and in the case of a country like El Salvador, with a very small initial enrolment, even as much as eightfold. Argentina, Uruguay and Chile do not present such startling growth figures, but this is because their secondary systems have for some years been better matched to the countries' needs (Havighurst and Abreu, 1962, p. 167).

In spite of this development, however, over the continent as a whole the enrolment represents only a small fraction of the age group. In Colombia in 1963 70,200 students, less than half of those who completed five years primary education, pursued their studies further, and since only 18 per cent of those who began finished the primary cycle, it is clear that the majority of children had finished with education by the age of twelve years. In 1962 Brazil had only 14 per cent of the population between the ages of twelve and eighteen years enrolled in post-primary schools, and was among those Latin American countries with the lowest percentage of secondary school enrolments, a long way behind Uruguay with 32 per cent, Argentina 31 per cent, or Chile and Venezuela with 23 and 21 per cent respectively. The south Brazilian littoral states ranked near to these countries, but their performance was offset by the poor enrolment record of the north-west and north-east regions, where over 92 per cent of the age group failed to attend secondary school, mainly because there are no teachers and no secondary schools. Of the 3,144 *municipios* in Brazil only 1,618 of them had secondary schools, and of these one thousand had no more than the first cycle and consequently could not offer direct entry into higher education. As in most Latin American states secondary education is essentially urban, the capitals concentrating 45 per cent of the student body within their boundaries. Guyana had 14 per cent of the age group in secondary high schools, excluding about three times this number who continued the first compulsory stage of their education up to the age of fourteen years in the post-primary section of all-age non-selective schools.

Private secondary schools

In short, secondary education is within reach of only a small fraction of the young people who might benefit from it. Lack of basic primary education, the economic position of the parents and the shortage of buildings and teachers make it unattainable for all except the urban middle classes. Though the State throughout Latin America lays down national programmes of study and claims the right of inspection, and in spite of increasing numbers of state schools, almost everywhere a good part of secondary education is still in private hands. Private profit is the purpose of some establishments, whose survival depends as much on the measure of their skill in evading ministerial regulations and the questioning of inspectors as on the quality of their educational service. Many are provided by religious bodies and indeed the Jesuits and other teaching orders were the pioneers of secondary education on the continent. In

Brazil over two-thirds of middle schools are in private hands. In Colombia 65 per cent of the academic secondary schools are private, 95 per cent of the commercial colleges and 55 per cent of the normal schools. In Mexico, even though participation of religious bodies was prohibited by the Constitution of 1917, there are now secondary schools run by organizations of the Church. In Guyana the principal secondary establishments, provided by the State, are supplemented by a few foundations of the Anglican and Catholic Churches, but at the same time there is a mushrooming of private academies.

Some private schools in Latin America were started in the hope of making a quick penny rather than from an ardent devotion to education. The schools owned by religious bodies had higher motives, a deep concern for educating the young being not always unmixed with more sectarian interests. Nearly all, however, provided a service in exchange for a fee, and sometimes quite a high fee. The position in this respect is not everywhere the same, and may be expected to improve with the growing awareness on the part of governments of their responsibilities in this sector of education. For example, in Brazil the introduction of grants-in-aid has enabled six hundred and forty independent non-state schools to participate in the Free Schools Campaign, and although only one-third of the schools are public, in 1962 six hundred thousand students were studying in academic secondary schools at public expense, as against less than five hundred thousand paying fees. In Mexico also in recent years there has been a substantial increase in the amount of public money made available for free secondary school places, and in Argentina secondary tuition in the public schools is free. It remains none the less true that for long the second stage of education was within reach of the pocket only of the privileged, and that this is generally so over much of the region. Free places are few. Colombia, for example, in 1962 offered just over ten thousand free places in official schools, of which over four thousand were for teachers in training. It is indeed not unknown for parents of children at private schools to resist official aid which might require the offer of free places on the grounds that children from families of low income would have an inferior cultural background and would lower the tone and standard of the schools.

The traditional curriculum

To say that because the schools charged fees they were constrained to supply what the customer demanded would be speaking excessively plainly. Nevertheless, reliance on fees has possibly perpetuated a tradition of secondary education which belonged to a select minority who felt themselves to be the heirs to positions of leadership, and at the same time to the culture of Europe. The secondary school has been a channel open to the few leading to the university, and with the requirements of the older type of higher study in mind, the contents of its courses and its methods of study followed the classical, humanist tradition. Such has been the prestige of the study of 'letters' that schools such as the *ginasios* of Brazil offering one cycle of four years' study only, insufficient to give entry to the university, adapted this type of curriculum, though it was not particularly suited as a preparation for other fields. The educational history of Guyana has been somewhat different, but the resultant situation is not unlike that in the neighbouring Latin territories. Secondary schools were certainly not restricted to a limited class; nevertheless, the official schools were founded by the colonial government to provide recruits for the civil service and later to train an élite to take over positions of authority when the administering power withdrew. It was, perhaps, inevitable that the model for the schools should be the traditional British 'public school', or the 'grammar school', with a mainly literary curriculum: there was no other lead at hand and the teachers who could be recuited were nurtured in that tradition. The need to measure achievement against some external standard made it equally inevitable that the curricula of the high schools should be determined by the requirements of the Cambridge Overseas School Certificate, so that the whole process of learning took place in a setting insulated from the stresses and needs of the students' own environment. Though the Guyanese secondary school has travelled by another route it has arrived at the same style of content as the *bachillerato* course.

Independence in Guyana did not find the philosophy behind limited entry into secondary education or the literary content particularly acceptable, but, on the contrary, released an insistent demand for expansion of the system to cater for three-quarters of the appropriate age group, and for reform of curricula in the light of the wider needs of national development. Similarly, elsewhere in the continent growing populations and the urgent need for economic expansion eroded the exclusiveness of post-primary education. The Latin American schools have not only sought to take in greater numbers but also to offer a variety of avenues into the working world other than the road to higher studies. Guyana's chosen path is the comprehensive school, with a curriculum covering commerce and scientific agriculture in addition to the normal grammar school subjects, together with a massive expansion of technical education. All Latin American countries responded to the international conference on secondary education held in Santiago de Chile in 1956 and looked at possible improvements. The tenth revision of the Colombian *bachillerato* in ten years was decreed in 1962 with the object of preparing 'the student to live in a society in constant evolution, as a result, among other factors, of changes in the cultural and social structure, scientific advances and technological progress'. At the same time as the reform sought to introduce scientific alternatives to the humanist course, it set out to make the secondary system an entry into intermediate careers as well as a channel to the university. It proposed to establish distinct levels in each type of school to meet the needs of the labour market, especially in the agricultural and industrial sectors, and to make each stage an end in itself.

Reform

In order to achieve these ends the Colombian reform laid down that the secondary school course should be in two cycles, and should embrace five disciplines – mathematics, Spanish, foreign languages, social studies and science, and religious and moral education. To this basic combination might be added artistic activities and specialization in certain fields which could prepare the pupil for his future career. The first cycle of studies would last four years and in its basic elements would be common to various types of secondary school, not only *bachillerato*, or grammar-type, but also to schools with an agricultural or industrial bias, and to teacher-training schools. The second cycle of two years would involve some specialization and would lead to the *bachillerato* certificate and to the university.

The Brazilian Basic Education Law of 1962 had similar intentions in respect of the academic secondary school system. The Federal Council of Education laid down the cycles for secondary education, the first, *ginasial*, lasting four years, and the second, *colegial*, of three or more years; it decided the length of the school year and minimum attendance requirements, and also specified certain compulsory subjects, including Portuguese, history, geography, mathematics and general science. The states were entitled to adapt the curricula to the needs of the area by including a number of appropriate optional subjects, of which English is one. Similar arrangements were made for the various kinds of vocational secondary school.

At the same time as reform is decreed, experimentation is going on to make the schools more responsive to the needs of the environment and of development. The Universidad del Valle in Colombia offers a typical example in its secondary school pilot project. This plan was the result of over five years co-operation with local academic schools during which the university offered evening and holiday courses to serving teachers. Four schools in the department with high-quality teaching staffs, good academic standards and efficient organization, were chosen as the locations for experimentation. Associated with each of them were up to five annexes – neighbouring schools which would develop within the limits of their resources along with the model schools. Both public and private schools were included among those selected. The project aimed to achieve its objects by bringing the expert knowledge of the university to the service of the schools. Attention was directed to five groups of study – languages, biological science, mathematics, natural science and the humanities – with a view to devising new methods and aids. Under the guidance of the Faculty of Humanities the teachers undertook a revision of the curricula laid down by the Ministry of Education in chemistry, biology, mathematics and physics in order to bring more flexibility into them. The use of simple basic laboratories constructed by the schools themselves were demonstrated. At the same time a start was made with providing libraries to the schools, and in training a staff member in library methods. The staffs of the schools involved were given special training courses to enable them to improve their professional competence, and to implement the plan efficiently. Ultimately the whole system of examinations and testing will be reviewed with a view to introducing changes which will encourage imaginative teaching and purposeful work by the students instead of rote learning. A second stage is envisaged during which a further six pilot schools, each with three annexes, will be brought into the scheme, and eventually it is hoped that the experiment will permeate the whole secondary system of the department, not only the *bachillerato* schools but also industrial, commercial, agricultural and normal schools, and indeed, that a form of comprehensive secondary school will evolve. The university has a special staff for the project, with a Director, seven auxiliary specialists in biology, chemistry, mathematics, physics, languages, social sciences and educational aids, together with a library specialist. Each school designates seven departmental heads who receive an additional honorarium, a librarian and a laboratory technician. The project has aroused considerable interest not to say envy among schools which have not been selected as pilot units. Finance, however, may jeopardize its effectiveness. The experiment has been undertaken with funds supplied by the Ford Foundation. The cost is 66,000 pesos annually for each school, and 300,000 for the university. While these sums are not enormous they are not negligible for the schools, and may prove more than the communities can raise when North American aid comes to an end. However, the signs are not entirely discouraging. Parents and former pupils have already shown themselves willing to lend support in money and effort, and the experiment could show that secondary schools can be established and financially maintained by communities in co-operation with the State.

Another Colombian innovation has been the *bachillerato nocturno*, the night-class *bachillerato* course, run at low cost on the premises of the day secondary schools, often using the same staff as well as the same equipment as the school. Similar multiple use of buildings and staff is seen in Brazil and other countries where separate schools are run in the mornings, afternoons and even also in the evenings.

Recently also Faculties of Education in Colombia, which are responsible for training secondary school teachers, have been putting their house in order. The third Seminar of Faculties of Education, which took place in Medellin in 1966, concentrated its efforts at looking at the objectives, organization and curricula of university departments of education, and all its recommendations were concerned with changes required to produce teachers whose training was up to date and in line with the needs of the country. The effects of this rethinking have yet to be seen, particularly in respect of increasing the supply of science teachers.

Vocational education

Parallel with the efforts to change the academic type of school went a growing concern with vocational secondary schools. Already there existed a number of schools within the secondary systems which were meeting special requirements in all the countries of the southern continent, although not unusually the courses offered were often less than four years of the basic cycle, and the schools were not in every case under the control of the Ministries of Education. There were numerous training centres similar to the Colombian *Escuelas de Práctico Agropecuarios* offering a two-year course leading to the certificate of *agricultor de Colombia* to sons of farmers who intended to follow agriculture as a livelihood; or the three-year course for women at a Nursing School leading to the qualification of 'rural nursing auxiliary'; or again the *Politecnos Complementarios* in country towns, which offered courses for the title of 'expert' in various feminine trades as well as training for those who wished to teach rural trades or play a part in community development. Similarly, in the larger towns elsewhere there was usually some provision for commercial and technical training, varying from country to country according to the national approach to the problems to be met, but many offering some basic qualification after a course of three or four years, and possibily after six years study a higher certificate such as the Colombian *bachiller técnico commercial.*

During the last decade or so there has been a new effort to extend facilities for vocational training and the provisions for industrial, agricultural and commercial schools in the 1962 Basic Education Law in Brazil are by no means isolated. The Brazilian *ensino medio tecnical* was to be organized in two cycles, just as in the academic type of secondary school. In the first cycle of four years, four subjects would be taught of which only one would be optional and the rest taken from the list of compulsory subjects of the academic course. In other words, the first cycle would be given over to general education. This general purpose would continue into the three years of the second cycle through five subjects taken from the usual academic *colegio* course, but technical subjects would also be introduced. Alternatively the programme of general subjects could be completed in one year's pre-technical course between the two cycles, leaving the students free to concentrate on the technical subjects alone at the *colegio* stage. These official courses might be provided in federal and state establishments, or in isolated centres in commercial and industrial enterprises.

Students of education and development have pointed out that the level of technical education in underdeveloped countries was poor and probably a waste of resources, and even in partially developed countries was not an efficient preparation for technological careers. The training provided in official secondary technical schools was often little valued by industry, because it seemed unrealistic and unrelated to the practices of the workshop floor, and out of step with immediate needs (Harbison and Myers, 1964). This has been true without doubt of some of the technical schools of Latin America, where laboratories are rare, equipment barely enough for demonstration by the teacher and hardly ever sufficient for the pupils to be able to conduct experiments. Some criticism could also be made of certain courses of the Technical Institute in Georgetown, Guyana, which even though backed by an Advisory Board with representatives of industry and trade unions has not always supplied satisfactory results. The reasons for this situation were generally lack of trained teachers coupled with lack of incentive offered to the middle-level technician as compared with the white-collar worker. Often, indeed, students pursued a technical education as a substitute for the unattainable academic course, just as in the past an aspirant to learning would enter a seminary in order to get some form of education. At the same time the industrialists and even government departments, failing to find suitably trained recruits in the official schools, would create their own training schemes to meet their own needs.

Although these strictures would apply to most of the vocational schools provided by the Ministry of Education in Colombia, the National Apprenticeship Service, SENA, organizes training centres which are almost of a different nature, in that they have been established after consideration of the real needs of the country, and not just in reponse to a theoretical need for technical instruction. During the first five years of its existence between 1958 and 1962 over fifty-nine thousand workers and apprentices followed courses at the centres of the *Servicio Nacional de Aprendizaje*, 3,697 in agriculture, 19,280 in manufacturing industry, 30,281 in commerce and 708 in transport. This figure fell short of the needs of the country, which amounted to some one hundred and ninety thousand workers each year, but it was impressive. SENA offers a wide variety of courses serving industry, commerce and agriculture. Some courses for young people are comparatively short and might be classified rather as elementary craft training. Others are within the sphere of adult training, giving the opportunity to older workers to bring their skills up to date and to make good the deficiencies of a purely on-the-job qualification, meeting special requests from enterprises to train supervisors and specialists, and also serving as an auxiliary technical training establishment for the armed forces. The basic apprenticeship courses, however, go beyond exclusively technical training and give a general secondary education. SENA's alumni are more than craftsmen; they are technicians who are filling a gap which has always existed between those trained on the workshop floor and the graduates from the universities. Colombia, like other Latin American countries, can boast four times as many administrators and professionals as people with intermediate qualifications, a situation the reverse of that in advanced countries, and quite incompatible with the demands of rapid development. SENA's main effort is a challenge to the traditional acceptance of two levels, the professional, doctor or engineer and the unskilled labourer. There are, however, prospects that SENA will not limit itself to the middle level of training but go beyond into the field of professional qualifications where the universities have no facilities as, for example, in foundry work. In 1965 SENA was working in eighteen centres in various parts of the country with a further twenty projected.

The success achieved by SENA may be attributed in considerable measure to its freedom from financial problems. Its source of income was assured by law from its inception by means of a levy equivalent to 1 per cent of the salary bill imposed on all undertakings with more than 100 million pesos capital or more than twenty workers. In 1963 this percentage was raised to 42 per cent and had to be paid by firms with more than 50 million pesos capital or more than ten workers. In addition the central government was required to contribute $\frac{1}{4}$ per cent of its salary bill from 1965 onwards to enable SENA to offer accelerated technical training to national service conscripts. As a result of these arrangements there was a steady improvement in the financial resources of SENA during its first six years. In 1958 just under ten thousand firms were contributing just under 2 million pesos: in 1963 more than three times that number of firms were participating to the extent of nearly 55 million pesos. During the same period the numbers trained rose from less than five thousand to about twenty thousand, and it is now expected that the new contributions will make it possible to double the number trained.

Because of their stake in SENA independent firms take a lively interest in its working. The firms maintain a 'master–apprenticeship' relationship with the students they send, and frequently make requests for particular training, either for apprentices or for older workers in need of new skills or reorientation. This kind of direct service to the customer is given not only to private enterprises but also to government departments: the armed forces particularly depend on SENA for training in some technical services. This immediate response to the needs of real conditions, which adequate financial resources backed by proper equipment and staff make possible, is one of the reasons for SENA's success. Another factor has been the effective co-operation it has enjoyed with certain international agencies, including the International Labour Office, and the Special Fund of the United Nations, as well as with the technologically advanced countries. The French Electricity Authority, for example, has collaborated in the training of craftsmen and technicians for the electricity producers, while the French metal and mechanical engineering industries have contributed to schemes in these fields. Britain is in process of setting up the first foundry school in Colombia, a project which will profoundly affect the methods of a host of small engineering firms throughout the country, and Spain, Germany and the United States also have agreements with SENA. Much of the credit, however, goes to the authorities of SENA itself. The service is organized on the basis of centralization of technical services and resources, and decentralization of administrative responsibility. The Central Directorate undertakes planning on both the short and the long term. Much of what has already been achieved has been based on detailed analysis of the manpower needs of the country, and on over seventy-five studies of occupations and operations in industry, agriculture, commerce, government and the services. The statistical data compiled by SENA, and also by the *Instituto Colombiano de Especialización Técnica en al Exterior*, ICETEX, ensure that the training plans in fact are relevant to the needs of the moment and contribute towards development. The analyses also point to activities for which centres will be required in the future: those projected on this basis include schemes for textile, graphic and commercial arts, naval construction, pharmaceutical chemistry, petro-chemistry, hotel and hospital services, banking and insurance, agricultural engineering and rural industries.

The idea of SENA came originally from Brazil where the twin *Servicio Nacional de Apprendizagem Industrial*, SENAI, and *Servicio Nacional de Aprendizagem Commercial*, SENAC, were established in 1942 to create a work force for industry which, it was hoped, would retain the population in the north-eastern states and so discourage emigration from the area to the cities of the south-east. The two services were run by associations of employers and were financed by a levy on firms. The Colombian success, however, has itself won recognition leading to imitation among neighbouring countries. Notably, Peru has followed the Colombian pattern in its National Apprenticeship and Industrial Labour Service, SENATI, which is an organization independent of government and supported by funds provided by manufacturers. A national centre has been established near Lima, and two regional centres at Chiclayo and Arequipa are planned. The buildings of the national centre are spaciously designed, and very well provided with equipment and facilities, including a modern auditorium with installations for film projection, instantaneous translation and closed-circuit television, as if to assign to technical training an importance which formerly it did not have. Visual aids for all courses are prepared in the centre printing shop by instructors who have specialized in this work. SENATI is concerned with all aspects of industrial training, including training within industry and reorientation and specialization courses for men already working in factories. The training in the national centre is designed with a practical bias, in various engineering trades, in diesel and motor workshop practices, welding and iron working, and a range of other industrial skills. The first three years of the courses covering four stages, pre-apprentice, basic, advanced and specialist, bring the student up to a standard of practical work equivalent to that of the City and Guilds Advanced Examination. There is some provision for general studies, including language, science, mathematics and engineering drawing, but the standard reached in these is distinctly lower. There are also facilities for sport. However, even though general education is not entirely neglected, the centre does not yet aspire to provide a general secondary technical education.

Obstacles to progress

In spite of experimentation and of progress on some fronts, nowhere has the implementation of reform been other than slow and difficult in the face of many obstacles. The average *colegio de bachillerato* remains much the same as it always was, possibly feeling that its curriculum is even more overloaded and all-embracing than in the past. The *bachiller* who completes the six-year course is all too often still incapable of independent work and thought, and has not acquired the habit of wide reading or of wise use of the library. One reason for the lack of progress in implementing change is clearly that a good proportion of schools are in private hands, and while the proprietors are not necessarily against official proposals, many of them have their own objectives, and nearly all have to find their own finance with no aid from official sources. They have not the means to introduce innovations and particularly they cannot retrain their staffs or recruit teachers with a fresh outlook, who are simply not available. It might be suspected that some of the religious bodies providing schools are not enamoured of some of the ideas of the government planners, among whom lay thinking predominates, and though the Minister usually issues programmes and has the right of inspection of schools, where he does not pay the piper he cannot easily get the tune changed.

Some of the explanation for poor achievement lies in the internal organization of the schools themselves. The rising tide of educational expectations is producing a flood of candidates for secondary education from the primary schools, so that the early forms of the existing schools are grossly overcrowded, in spite of the shift system commonly in force which spreads the pressure over the whole day.

In Colombia only eleven thousand out of the twenty-eight thousand applicants for entry into the first year of the state schools could be accepted in 1963. Everywhere the position is much worse for girls, even though fewer of them seek places, and much worse in rural areas, because of the uneven geographical distribution of schools. Yet, although the secondary sector is growing throughout the continent, many schools find it difficult to maintain the desirable rate of growth in the later forms because of wastage. The example of Brazil is typical. Of every one thousand students who entered the second grade of education at the age of twelve years, only 115 completed four years of study, only fifty-five seven years and no more than twenty-three survived to reach the level of higher education. Wastage is generally worse in the few scattered secondary schools in the rural areas, probably because the farms demand the labour of young people, while in the town employment is not so readily available. Distances provide a further problem which is not so acute in urban centres. In Colombia wastage is more serious in the official schools than in the private. This seems somewhat paradoxical at first glance since the government schools though not free are much less expensive. The explanation is that the poorer parent cannot hope to send his children to private schools, but he will make heroic sacrifices to obtain an education for them, even to the extent of never spending money on meat for himself or of frankly starving himself to keep up the payments. Not infrequently it does prove impossible, especially when costs rise as they usually do. Rising costs are a universal headache for the South American parent, particularly as incomes rarely rise at the same pace. A common illustration of this problem arises out of the normal practice of using private school buses for transporting the children to and from school. The bus charges are substantial to start with. As the pressure on places increases and the accommodation in the centre of the towns becomes both inadequate and a valuable asset to dispose of in periods of rapid city development, schools are seeking new sites on the outskirts or even beyond the built-up areas. Moves outwards naturally increase the transport costs which are particularly onerous for those on modest incomes. Faced with ever-increasing expenses the indigent parent cannot continue to deprive himself of the wage capacity of the children.

The supply and training of teachers

The low standards achieved have their origin in the poor basis of primary education, but they are being aggravated by the increased pressures on the secondary level, the dearth of materials, textbooks, libraries and other aids, and their poor quality. Above all, the teaching methods are frequently obsolete and imperfectly assimilated. Too often there is really no teaching at all but dictating of notes and parrot learning. This is not surprising as many schools are staffed almost entirely by unqualified teachers.

The regular training of teachers for secondary schools in Brazil is conducted in the Faculties of Philosophy, Science and Letters of the universities in a four-year course, which includes special study of the subjects to be taught as well as pedagogical training. Teachers who aim to take up posts in secondary technical schools follow special courses. *Colegios de Aplicão*, practice schools, form an integral part of the university, and the staffs are members of the faculty. This makes it possible to integrate theory and practical training with excellent results, which cannot be matched by the British method of training secondary school teachers. However, only about 20 per cent of the total number actually teaching in Brazilian secondary schools have qualifications from these faculties. The majority are products of the normal schools, or have trained for some profession other than that of teaching, such as the law, or have no academic qualifications at all. In Colombia the Faculties of Education have the duty to train the *professores de bachillerato*, but they are not supplying sufficient numbers. In 1963 there were 2,652 qualified men and 843 women teaching *bachillerato* courses, against twice these numbers with no more than a secondary school education as qualification. In particular the schools have not been able to get teachers of science. Only about a quarter of those teaching science had appropriate qualifications, and to meet the needs of the next ten years the annual production of science graduate teachers would have to rise to 380, an increase of over 100 per cent. This is certainly typical of the less well-developed countries, though Argentina and Chile have fewer difficulties in recruiting trained people. Unfortunately, where the need for development is greatest very few of the body of secondary teachers could be described as strongly motivated by a sense of vocation, and few again of those who would escape this stricture would be capable of changing their outlook and rewriting their courses to fall more in line with modern pedagogical thought.

Mediocre standards are related to the poor status and salary of secondary school masters, which do not compare well with those of other professions. The rewards in the schools are not everywhere adequate to provide a reasonable standard of living for a man and his family, and the secondary teacher may be faced with the choice of taking a second job during his free time, or seeking better-paid employment than teaching. The situation of the Guyanese teacher is not appreciably better, except in the government schools where the salary scales have been patterned on the European rates of colonial times. Even the official schools in the circumstances immediately following Independence had to face competition for the services of the local graduate, a relatively scarce commodity with opportunities open to him for high appointment in the administrative and political fields, where the rewards in salary and status were far higher than could be offered by the schoolmaster's profession. The Guyana Development Plan estimated that something approaching four hundred graduates would be required every year, at least up to 1971, half of the number in agriculture, engineering, medicine and the natural sciences. Even assuming that all those studying abroad would return to Guyana, the current output of university-trained manpower falls a long way short of the total required. Education's chances of continuing to take its fair proportion cannot be reckoned to be very bright. Similarly, in those Latin countries which are embarking on steep economic expansion it is not easy to be optimistic about the chances of the middle-level schools in the competition for university educated people.

Radio and television

In order to offset the shortage of trained teachers and also to make good the dearth of secondary schools in rural areas, at the beginning of 1968 Mexico inaugurated a nation-wide scheme for broadcasting television lessons. Unlike Colombia, which started educational television at the first stage, Mexico gave priority to the second, on the grounds that while almost every village had a primary school, secondary schools were lacking over wide areas. The broadcasting of the first year of the secondary course began after extensive experimentation with closed circuit television within the Department of Audio-visual Education in the Federal Ministry, and was limited to the central states of Veracruz, Puebla, Hidalgo, Morelos, Guerero and Mexico State. The usual secondary school programme is followed for six hours daily from Monday to Friday with a further three hours on Saturdays. The broadcasts are received in special rooms created in villages where no secondary school exists. Each room, or *tele-aula* as it is called, is in charge of a single master who has twenty or thirty students registered. The master receives special training to equip him to supervise work in all subjects included in the televised lessons. In the course of time the scheme will be extended to cover the whole country, and all six years of the secondary course.

There is clearly a long way to go before the *tele-aulas* can be integrated into the cultural life of the countryside and make a real contribution to its development. The fact that the usual curriculum is followed may simply prepare intelligent young people for work in the city and increase the movement from the country. Even in urban areas educational television at secondary level is still in its infancy, however, and has not yet been able to relieve the pressure on the traditional system. The failure to achieve any appreciable improvement in the standards of secondary education is explained in part by the tremendous effort at expansion which has put an added strain on resources already stretched. Growth certainly has been set in motion, but not so effectively in the non-academic sectors as to offer a genuine choice of alternative avenues through the second stage of education into the world of work. In Brazil the fastest rate of growth in 1962 was in the normal school, followed closely by the commercial, and again by the academic. However, since the academic sector started with nearly six times the number of students as the commercial, which was next in order of enrolment, in actual increased numbers the academic school was far ahead. By any reckoning the industrial and agricultural schools trailed a long way behind (Havinghurst and Abreu, 1962). Looking at enrolments in Brazil, 1962 statistics show that in the first cycle over 83 per cent of students were in academic schools, as compared with just over 2 per cent for industrial schools. The academic *ginasio* clearly produced recruits for the second cycle of other branches, as at this stage its proportion dropped to 41 per cent, and the commercial and normal shares rose to 31 and 24 per cent respectively. The industrial percentage, however, remained low at 3·6 per cent. In Colombia in the same year the proportions in the various branches followed the same order as in Brazil, though the industrial sector had a somewhat larger share of the enrolment.

Motives and priorities

This slowness on the part of the second stage of education to adapt itself to the policy of diversification reveals a conflict of purpose between the educational and economic planners and the parents. The secondary school is traditionally the means whereby the middle classes preserve their social status and safeguard the future generation against the encroachments of the untamed forest and mountain, and such is the prestige which even now illuminates the study of 'letters' that sections of the population which formally did not aspire to learning now seek in the *bachillerato* a path to higher social and economic standing. The parents are consumers whose thoughts are dominated by the wish to keep up with the neighbours. The planners, on the other hand, are production engineers trying to match the product to the indications of the market surveys. SENA's investigation into the training needs of Colombia indicated the chronic shortages of skilled technicians and of specialist training institutions at the secondary level. In 1963 the Colombian Institute for Advanced Training Abroad initiated a nation-wide study to determine the relationship between education and development in Colombia and in the final report, which contained an analysis of the educational system, pin-pointed the urgent need to develop specialist training facilities in a more diversified secondary system. Starting from the conviction that human skill and knowledge are as important as capital formation and physical resources, the report relates education and economic development: both form part of an integral process. Few parents in Colombia or elsewhere understand, or even know about this informed and specialist point of view. They continue to go for what appeared best in their younger

63

days. For the time being the parents are winning in the conflict of motives and priorities.

Argentina, the sole economically advanced country of the southern continent, may claim to have developed a secondary education system adequate in size and in diversity of function for its needs. In the countries approaching the advanced stage, Mexico, Venezuela, Chile, Uruguay and Costa Rica, are tackling the problem created by the flood of primary school leavers seeking to continue their studies at the next stage, and may be within sight of a solution. They have not, however, yet approached adequate specialist diversification of the secondary school to meet the needs for trained manpower. The partially developed countries, which must include Colombia, Peru, Paraguay, Ecuador and parts of Brazil, have not reached a satisfactory point either quantitatively, or in the degree of diversification required. In these countries secondary education should have the largest claim, in the view of Harbison and Myers, on expenditure for education, even up to 40 per cent of the total funds available, though none of them are anywhere near doing so. Some parents and planners would agree with ministers of education on the desirability of enabling every child without distinction of origin to enjoy secondary education, in order to achieve the highest cultural and professional level that his aptitudes and personality justify. The Latin American world offers few examples of this being a reality.

5
Higher education

More than one hundred and fifty universities exist at the present time in the nineteen Latin American republics. The University of Saint Thomas Aquinas in Santo Domingo opened its doors in 1538, when the Pope authorized the Dominican friars to found four faculties, Theology, Law, Arts and Medicine, in the style of the University of Salamanca. Even in those early days there was a fore-token of later shortages of highly qualified teachers; there were not enough doctors in the new world to enable medicine to be taught and the faculty was a non-starter. Not deterred, however, by the formidable difficulties of settling an unknown continent the early colonizers did not neglect interests of the mind, and before the sixteenth century had run its course there were universities in Mexico, Peru and Colombia. During the following two centuries more appeared, in Argentina and Chile; three in Peru, San Cristobal de Huamanga and the University of Ayacucho, both founded in 1677, and San Antonio de Abad at Cuzco; as well as several others in Venezuela, Ecuador and Bolivia. Up to this time the universities were mainly religious foundations. The rectors were priests, and their function was to train priests to carry out the civilizing work that the Church had set itself in the Americas. Teaching orders were naturally particularly to the fore in establishing centres: the Dominicans, first in the field, in time were overhauled in the extent of their work by the Jesuits, who founded the university in Mexico City, and San Marcos in Lima in 1551, the Colegio de Córdoba in 1611, the Javeriana in Colombia in 1622, and Santiago de Chile, and Chuquisaca in Bolivia in 1624.

Some of the early universities have survived to this day and have a continuous tradition at least as long as many European foundations. By the end of the eighteenth century, however, the missionary zeal which had impelled the Church to offer the blessings of European civilization to the indigenous peoples had all but spent itself. The mission failed in the face of the insistent demand of succeeding generations of creole landowners and officials for education befitting their positions. The University of San Gregorio in Quito, one of the most successful and conservative centres of the Spanish empire, so lost sight of the ideal of service to the whole community as to require student applicants to give evidence of purity of blood and of an ancestry undefiled by indulgence in trade. Some universities disappeared permanently or for long periods. The University of San Fulgencio also in Quito, after nearly two hundred years of existence, was suppressed in 1786, somewhat surprisingly for academic inefficiency, later to be absorbed into the Central University. The Jesuit colleges did not fully recover from the expulsion of the Society from Brazil in 1759, and from the Spanish dominions in 1767, even when they were permitted to renew their activities in 1814. By this time, the influence of the English philosophers and the French encylopaedists, of freemasonry and the French revolution had revived a secular and anti-clerical tradition in higher education which went back to the Islamic universities of Spain. The liberally inclined protagonists of independence, realizing the need to replace the departed imperialist administrators and, like the rulers of the new states of recent days, not unmindful of the value of universities as symbols of national prestige, founded new seats of learning everywhere. Even the conservative 'junta', which started the movement of 10 April 1810 in Venezuela, within five months of the coup re-established the University of the Andes at Merida. The University of Buenos Aires dates from 1821, five years after the Argentine declaration of independence. Bolívar himself decreed the foundation of universities at Cartagena in Colombia, and Trujillo and Arequipa in Peru, and shortly afterwards Santander had a plan for starting new universities in Bogotá, Caracas and Quito, as well as for establishing a national museum in the colonial prison and a national library, both of which still prosper in Bogotá. After the first fine enthusiasm, the rest of the nineteenth century was a period of violent political upheaval during which the heirs to Spanish and Portuguese rule struggled for the seats of power and cared little for learning, and less for the social conditions of the mass of the people. A few universities were indeed opened. Only one of these, the Catholic University of Chile which started in 1888, was a religious foundation. The rest owed their existence to the State, and some closed for reasons of state. In 1876 the Peruvian Government suspended the universities at Trujillo, Ayacucho and Puno in order to provide funds for the armed forces. The history of the University of Uruguay well illustrates the trend. Founded in the eighteen-thirties under the auspices of the Government, it came under some Church influence and developed a measure of independence from the State. By the middle of the century the anti-clericals had fought back and carried the day, and by 1885 the university was firmly established as a state institution, controlled by the rector nominated by the Government, with no rivals in the field of higher education.

By the end of the nineteenth century a pattern of Latin American university education was clear. The background was provided by the religious foundations which had survived. On this ground were laid the secular institutions, generally more or less anti-clerical in outlook. Law, the most useful professional qualification for the sons of the oligarchs, had ousted theology as the main subject of study, and in the new Externado University, just as in the ancient Colegio Mayor de Nuestra Señora de Rosario in Bogotá, was virtually the only course offered. Service to the community had ceased to be a conscious objective of either the teachers or the taught, and scientific research, which had been a feature of the previous century, had had no chance to evolve as a university function in the turbulent conditions of the age. It was generally accepted that the main purpose of the university was to prepare students for the learned professions, as a means of inculcating the values and standards proper to their class and to the positions of authority they expected to inherit. With the onset of the next century the modern world of technology began to encroach on the isolation of the university and higher education was reshaped under new pressures and influences. Military dictators such as Generals Juan Vicente Gómez and Marco Pérez Jiménez in Venezuela may have impeded the smooth process of adjustment even for as long as thirty years, but on their demise the path of rational evolution was inevitably taken up again. It was not until the twentieth century that Brazil developed university institutions.

Growth of technical studies

The most evident new departure was towards technical studies. Even before the turn of the century a technical university was opened at the Bolivian mining and railway centre, Oruro, and at the present time not one of the republics is without a faculty of engineering if not a full technological university. Colombia, though more generously endowed with institutions of higher education than many of its neighbours, is not exceptional in the shape of its university pattern. Within the capital, alongside the traditional schools of law, have grown several institutions with a different bias: the Universities of America and Gran Colombia founded in 1951 have schools of engineering of various kinds. The University of Bogotá founded in 1954 specializes in cartography and topography, statistics and administration, and maintains a high-altitude biological institute. In 1949 the new University of the Andes opened its engineering schools and worked out a close relationship with various North American universities: after completing their first five semesters in Bogotá, engineering students went to Illinois, Maine, Michigan, Arizona, New Mexico, Kansas or to the Massachusetts Institute of Technology to complete their bachelor's degree. This scheme enabled 'the Andes' to concentrate on the work of the early years to good effect, so that now the majority of students complete their degrees in Bogotá and graduate as some of the best-trained engineering specialists on the continent. In 1952 the *Universidad Distrital* started courses in forestry and electronic engineering, and while the new institutions were emerging the National University was steadily building up its technological faculties. The same developments were taking place in the provincial cities, the older foundations adding technical studies to their traditional curricula, while new universities concentrated entirely on the technical fields of study. The century-and-a-half-old University of the Cauca at Popayan added telecommunications to its faculties a decade or so after the Industrial University of Santander opened in Bucaramanga in 1948 with a full range of engineering studies. Last in the arena in 1960 appeared the Technological University of Pereira.

The growth of new institutions with modern programmes of study has resulted in some marked changes in the choice of specialization made by students. Until recently in Colombia the favourite fields were medicine, civil engineering and law, but since 1955 the traditional studies have given way before a rising tide of interest in the pure and applied sciences, the social sciences and in education. Between 1952 and 1963 the body of university students doubled from just over seven thousand to nearly fifteen thousand. At the beginning of the decade medicine and law topped the graduation table with 34 and 26 per cent respectively. Education, social sciences and agriculture all had less than 5 per cent of the graduates produced, while the exact sciences together had only 7·6 per cent. At the end of the period medicine and law were still the favourite subjects, but their proportion of graduates had gone down to 18 per cent, to the benefit mostly of the social sciences, agriculture, education and the various forms of engineering other than civil (ICETEX, 1966).

In the technical fields university studies led normally to graduate professional qualifications, but at the same time some courses were designed to meet the growing needs for technically trained people at the middle level of skill, whom the modern sector of the economy was failing to get from the secondary schools. To some observers this would appear to be a falling-off from standards, and indeed the whole inclination towards the technical and undesirable deviation from what was proper to a university. Nevertheless, the trend is in line with what is happening elsewhere. During the last decade of British rule Guyana shared the facilities of the University of the West Indies, which was established on the British model in 1949. At that time the British definition would not have admitted many institutions accepted as universities in Latin America which provided no more than vocational courses. The British university claimed that its primary task was to educate rather than simply to prepare for a profession. The university in Jamaica reflected this definition, and at the same time accepted the high entry standards, together with the dedicated quality of teaching and low student failure rates, which were the justification for selective entry, and also the concept of a small university campus housing a community of scholars seeking truth primarily for its own sake. The creation of the University of Guyana in 1963 was not unconnected with the political platform of the ruling party of the day, and with the pursuit of a symbol of independence, but the move revealed also an uneasiness at the slow progress made in the training of specialists who were essential for development. The Guyana Development Plan envisaged the university adding technical training to its facilities for tuition in arts, natural science and social sciences, and spoke of an Institute of Education, which would take over responsibility for training primary teachers, an Agricultural Faculty, based on the existing Guyana

School of Agriculture, and an Engineering School which would offer technological and possibly also technician courses. There would now probably be little dispute that this experimentation in adjusting the higher education structure to the changed perspective of the modern age is vital, and that Guyana and the Latin countries are interpreting their situation realistically. At the same time they are not out of step with the trend of thought in other parts of the world, including Britain, where the upgrading of the colleges of advanced technology is recognition that they have the same intellectual standards as traditional universities.

Vocational and liberal education

The reshaping of the content of courses in the image of the technological era did not fundamentally modify the vocational role of the Latin American university. More varied specialist disciplines supplemented law, medicine and civil engineering, but their function remained preparation for positions of leadership and management. The horizons of the specialist courses were, if anything, narrower, but their very narrowness stimulated the corrective. The average freshman came up familiar with a wide range of subjects, but lacking in essential basic knowledge, particularly in the sciences, to begin a highly specialized course, and, though possibly a skilled memorizer, was more often than not unversed in methods of independent study and scientific thinking. Universities had no choice but to give their students the general preparation necessary for their professional courses. The *colegio universitario*, created by Brazilian universities, sets out to make good the deficiencies in method from which the average school student suffers on embarking on higher studies. In Mexico the candidate for a university professional qualification may undertake courses of general studies before being admitted to the specialist programme. The *Instituto Tecnologico y de Estudios Superiores* of Monterrey sets out to train scientists and engineers 'conscious of their responsibilities to society and their fellow human beings', and to avoid the dangers of an exclusively technological training. Students first enter the *Escuela Preparatoria* where they pursue general studies, including particularly languages, and have the opportunity to develop their own methods of study through private reading and research, laboratory work and discussion with their teachers. The Colombian University of the Andes in Bogotá has shown a similar awareness of the need to balance technical and professional training with liberal studies. The Andes, which was founded by a group of young intellectuals as an institution independent of both political and confessional influence, set out to graft on to the Latin American vocational tradition the liberal education characteristic of the North American and European systems, producing the professional specialists with a solid humanistic background, cultured men conscious of their obligations to society. All students entering the university are required to follow courses of general studies in the Faculty of Arts and Sciences, and to continue this general education after they have started to work in their specialist field. The objects of the general courses are to give the student the knowledge of basic subjects necessary for his professional studies and to teach him to study and think independently by means of laboratory work, participation in seminars, by the use of the library and by field work. The minimum general course is normally completed within the first two years at the university, but general studies may be continued after specialization has begun. The Faculty of Arts and Sciences is consequently not simply another faculty, but, offering special services to all the departments of the university and in touch with all the students, has a unique function as a link between the parts and as an animator of discussion. The University of the Andes would attribute the singular success it claims for its policy partly to the decision to limit enrolment to an ultimate maximum of two thousand students.

Though exceptionally well pursued, the schemes are not unique, and many universities, even the very large institutions, have felt obliged to attempt something of this nature. Indeed, growing enrolment has been a factor in directing attention to reorganizing the programmes of general studies. The *Escuelas de Idiomas*, to be found in many universities, have replaced the small language classes which previously the various faculties set up for their own purposes, and have made efficient teaching of foreign languages to increasing numbers of students possible, if not always a reality. Similarly, with the shortage of teachers and equipment instruction in basic sciences suffers if the various faculties are left to provide themselves with what they need, and consequently the kind of general service to all faculties offered in mathematics, physics, chemistry and biology by four specialist institutes of the University of Concepción in Chile finds favour in other centres of higher studies.

The ideal balance of technical and liberal studies and the integration of faculties and departments, which may be attainable in a small and new university, have to be sacrificed in the university which over a period of years has built up a varied pattern of teaching institutions and very large numbers of students. The *Universidad Nacional Autónoma de Mexico*, UNAM, after over fifty years of existence has now over fifty thousand students. Its faculties and schools have remained separate and even isolated, the buildings and facilities of one institution, for example, not being available to another, as happens in the Technological Institute of Monterrey. Sheer size explains this to a large extent. However, some of the explanation lies in the course of development of the university. Its foundation was preceded in 1910 by the creation of the School of Advanced Studies with the particular object of fostering higher studies and research, especially in science. Later in the same year this was amalgamated with the existing Schools of Jurisprudence, Medicine, Engineering and Fine Arts to form the National University. By 1929 there were ten faculties including Social Sciences, Dentistry, Commerce and Administration, Music, Veterinary Medicine, Law, Medicine, Science and Architecture. The National Library and the National Observatory were also within the university. These parts were added at different times and maintained a good measure of separateness. Although to be recognized degree courses have to be registered with the Mexican Government, the content is prescribed largely by the individual faculties and schools; the courses are for the most part obligatory and offer little scope for choice. Recently there has been an effort to reduce the overcrowding of the curricula and to make some choice available. The means suggested is the 'credit system' whereby courses are given numerical values and the student can make a selection to reach a required total of points, as opposed to following required subjects (Bonn, 1963). In the face of the very large numbers of students and the separate interests of the faculties and schools, these changes have not yet made much progress. Size, however, has encouraged the development of modern techniques which may in due course help to penetrate the barriers: recently the Faculty of Dentistry has introduced comprehensive closed-circuit television to extend the range of the lecture, and to improve the contact between the teacher and student.

In the course of its development UNAM has evolved a unique pattern of higher studies which has become characteristic of Mexican university organization. The university has three kinds of consti- tuent institution: the schools, the faculties and the research insti- tutes. The schools teach professional courses leading to the first degree of 'lawyer', 'engineer' and so on; the curriculum, which covers five years, restricts itself to scientific, technical and practical vocational subjects. This type of first degree work is also done in technical fields in the schools of the National Polytechnic Institute, which comes under the authority of the Federal Secretary of Education. In the Polytechnic, however, it is done side by side with middle-level vocational training which is offered in secondary vocational and pre-vocational schools, and a Commercial High School and an Industrial High School. In the university the faculties work at a higher level than the schools, offering advanced degrees for which students must perform individual research. The research institutes concentrate on original research both in the humanities and in science.

The university and the community

In another way the National University of Mexico is remarkable. The new buildings, erected mainly during the presidency of Miguel Aleman, are impressive for their grandeur and beauty. Combining artistic motifs derived from the art of ancient Mexico with the functional efficiency of modern materials and architectural design, the campus is *par excellence* the national symbol of faith in education.

A feature, common to both small and large universities, is the growing number of women students. Women increasingly partici- pate as equals with the men in the academic and social life of the campus. While industry and commerce have attracted female labour into offices and shops from families of modest means, new oppor- tunities for professional careers for girls have also emerged. Within a generation middle-class families have ceased to look upon a good marriage as the only career for their daughters and have begun to entertain the possibility of alternatives. They have been willing to pay fees for them, just as for the sons, and to support the girls' secondary schools, and even mixed secondary schools, in order to permit them to proceed to professional studies. The girl who has fully emancipated herself from her family and maintains her independence on her secretary's salary may still be rare, but more and more girls are seeking university training, principally in the humanities as teachers, but also, threatening male preserves, as lawyers, doctors, even engineers and metallurgists. Some universities have welcomed this change because it was thought that women, being naturally more attached to the basic family virtues, would have a stabilizing influence on student life which would work against riot and disorder. And almost all view the development with favour because a mixed community on the campus is more typical of the community at large, and a better setting for preparation for life.

The development of technical studies, the attention paid to general knowledge and the growing participation of women, may be interpreted as responses to the claims of the changing world in which the universities are working. Instances are also not lacking in recent years of more conscious assumption of the role of service to the community. In the north of South America this effort has been directed less towards the creation of extra-mural extension services than to fostering social studies, and especially those bearing on local and continental problems. The Institute for Technological and Higher Studies at Monterrey in Mexico offers a typical example of the way the work is arranged. There is no specific extension department. All the schools of the university, such as the School of Agriculture and Animal Husbandry, are free to organize courses, issue bulletins to disseminate the results of research, and to make specialist advice available beyond the campus. In addition there are several societies whose function is in part to provide a link between the university and the community. The *Sociedad Artística Tecnológico* and the *Departamento de Difusión Cultural* arrange concerts, exhibitions, cinematograph shows and theatrical performances; the Department of Industrial Relations and the Institute for Industrial Research offer specialist services to industry, and public bulletins and reviews; and the university television station provides a cultural service to various sections of the population of Monterrey. The University of the Andes in Colombia also offers an example of effective initiative on these lines in its Centre of Economic Development, which in addition to its academic programme of work, has undertaken specific research projects for both government and private enterprise. Also in Bogotá the Faculty of Social Science at the National University has placed particular emphasis on research into the Colombian situation, and in its Graduate School of Sociology into Latin American problems. The Department of Economic Planning, which has for some time been shared by the Universities of Cartagena and Atlántico in Colombia, has directed its attention to the economic backwardness of the region, and will play a major role in the future in a scheme, sponsored by the Organization of American States, for a four-part federal university, incorporating two new universities of Córdoba and of Magdalena; the federal university is expected to make a decisive contribution in research and expertise to the economic development of the Caribbean coastal area. At the other end of the continent in Argentina and Chile, where the social role is more explicit and more developed, most universities have some form of extension services, and also undertake schemes such as the recent project of the University of Buenos Aires which made the guidance of social science and agricultural specialists available to workers settling near the capital after migration from the interior. The University of Concepción, under an agreement with the Chilean Development Corporation, has contributed to economic studies, which have helped the planning of regional development. Again in Chile the Catholic University of Valparaiso gives a unique example of sustained service to the community in the programmes of its private television station devoted to fundamental and adult education.

Further opportunities to employ university resources in the service of the community are offered where associations of universities exist. The Central American University Higher Council is able to take steps through its technical commission for regional planning to make the most effective use of higher education resources in meeting the needs of the region. The University of San Carlos in Guatemala provides a practical illustration of this co-operation in the joint educational research programme which it manages on behalf of neighbouring universities in El Salvador, Nicaragua, Costa Rica and Honduras, with the help of the Agency for International Development and Michigan State University. The Colombian Association of Universities, which came into being following the recommendation of the 1957 National Congress of Universities, also gives valuable services to all state and private recognized universities of the country. They range from the purely domestic, such as the pharmacy and bookshop, to surveys of national graduate manpower requirements. After publishing a short-term plan for university expansion in 1965, it invited an international team to co-operate with it in a fuller investigation with a view to suggesting the best use of Colombia's resources of higher education to correspond with the country's future development. This project was completed in 1967.

Research

Outside the province of the social sciences, in the less developed countries the universities have not carried out much research. Where such work has been called for it has been undertaken by organizations especially established such as the Colombian Institute for Technological Research, the research stations of the Ministry of Agriculture, or in independent centres such as the internationally known philological Institute *Caro y Cuervo*, which is carrying out a language survey of Colombia. However, the position is changing. Established universities are beginning to pay more attention to fundamental research, and some of the newer ones gave it high priority from the moment of inauguration. The sponsors of the *Universidad del Oriente*, for example, six years before it was founded in 1960, planned an Oceanographic Institute as part of the university with the support of the Venezuelan Foundation for the Advancement of Science. Scholarships to enable prospective members of staff to be trained were offered, abroad because there were no facilities within the country. The Institute now concentrates its research on the physical chemistry, geology, biology and fishing problems of the Gulf of Cariaco, which offers prospects of a thriving fishing industry in the future. Many of the senior staff are Venezuelan born, though a good deal of reliance has still to be placed on overseas experts who bring their knowledge of special fields from Norway, Germany, Canada, Chile and the United States.

In the south, in Argentina and Chile universities have developed research activities further in every field. Some of this research, for example in animal husbandry in the University de la Plata and in soil science in the University of the South, might in other territories be carried out by government research stations. The same observations could be made about the research projects into corn cultivation, the fattening of cattle, and artificial insemination being conducted by the Agrarian University of Peru. In Chile there are some forty university research centres in receipt of government grants for work in such varied fields as astronomy, physics, biology, medicine, music and the plastic arts.

University reform

Though the developments do not reach a uniformly high level, they do indicate a certain renewed vitality in the realm of higher education. There is, however, another aspect of university affairs in Latin America during the twentieth century which has attracted public attention much more dramatically than purely academic matters. The University Reform Movement was launched into the world in 1918 when the 'Argentine youth of Córdoba' issued a 'Manifesto to the Free Men of South America'. There were in fact three lines of thought in this proclamation and not all of them were new. Some of the clauses called for the kind of developments just described, the introduction of new subjects and methods, of liberal as well as professional programmes, the involvement of the university in national social problems. The desired changes had in fact already begun, and continued to gather momentum as the century proceeded. A plea for academic freedom, for appointments solely on the grounds of academic merit were contained in a second group of provisions, which constituted a protest in the name of university autonomy against political manipulation of institutions of higher education. Freedom to teach and think in complete immunity from the influences of the time was always an ideal too refined for attainment in the workaday world of Latin America, and the Youth of Córdoba were not really proposing such ivory-towered isolation. The protest was rather against attempts of the oligarchs to restrict higher education, and against practices which had arisen during the political upheavals of the previous centuries; the convenient compromises reached then between the politicians who sought power and the university authorities who needed funds began to look tawdry to a fresh generation of youthful idealists. There were in the claim for autonomy elements of an earlier tradition dating back to the first days of the conquest, when the concept, derived from the University of Bologna, of a corporation of students served by teachers, was still alive. Yet, even then it is doubtful whether an autonomous company of scholars dedicated to the pursuit of learning ever existed in South America. The earliest universities were religious foundations, subject to the purposes and discipline of the Order which administered them, and amenable to the decisions of the Church hierarchy. Evidence of the degree of control which could once be exercised persists still to these days in, for example, the Pontifical University of Rio de Janeiro, whose Rector is nominated by the Archbishop and who can overrule decisions of the University Council which are passed by less than a two-thirds majority, or in the Catholic University of Peru, whose statutes call for conformity with the laws of the State, but also for absolute obedience to the Holy See to which the University is subordinate. The cause of university autonomy was, nevertheless, a worthy one, and was pursued vigorously and effectively over the whole continent. University government is now fairly generally vested in three organs of the university itself, although the Colombian Decree 1297 of 1964 was not unique in retaining for the central government the ultimate authority through regulations and directives and the right of inspection. The supreme authority to approve statutes, create schools and faculties, and to elect the Rector rests with the University Assembly, as it is usually called, though it can have other names, as does the *Consiliatura* of the National University of Colombia. The academic policy-making body is the University Council, and the executive organ is the Rector and his staff. The faculties are organized on parallel lines. Constitutionally the autonomy of the university organs of government is complete, with the exception of those religious universities over which the Church hierarchy exercises an overriding authority. In practice, the manner in which the universities make use of their power is influenced to a great extent by the composition of the Councils, by the form of election of the Rector and by the terms under which they receive their income.

The three parts of the university community are normally represented on the councils and assemblies: the teaching staff, the alumni and the students, in varying proportions. In official universities in Chile, Paraguay and Uruguay, and in private institutions generally the whole of the teaching body, the *claustro*, sit in the Assembly; in the rest representatives of the professors sit together with the delegates of the other estates. In Chile there is no student representation at this level; in the Colombian *Consiliatura* students are weakly represented, and their influence is counterbalanced by the presence of representatives of government, the Church and the parents, who stand for stability, or even, some would say, for reaction in times of crisis. The Assembly elects the Rector, usually for a limited period of time, presumably to prevent him outstaying his welcome and becoming too powerful. Long tenure of office has little attraction, however, to not a few rectors, who appear anxious to go before their time: of eight rectors elected in Argentine in 1957 only three were still in office in 1960. Private institutions seem to be more successful in holding on to their principals.

Similarly, the University Councils have multiple representation. The deans of the faculties, and possibly a few other teaching personnel, have a seat, together with representatives of the alumni and students. The Council of the National University of Chile also has officials from the cabinet of the President of the Republic and the Ministry of Education, and while it does have student members they have no vote.

Financing of higher education

The methods of financing universities vary throughout the southern continent. In Argentina 95 per cent of the funds of the National University are derived from the Federal Budget. No income at all is derived from student fees, even foreign students being given free tuition. On the other hand, state support to private universities is forbidden by law. They depend on the contributions of their supporters, on student fees and also on grants from the great North American foundations. The position is more favourable to private institutions in Chile, where national grants make up 50 per cent of their budgets. The National University of Chile depends for 70 per cent of its funds on the State, and on private contributions and student fees for the rest. In Peru the official universities receive government grants by monthly instalments, and also the proceeds of the alcohol tax, while the Catholic University has no state aid but meets 62 per cent of its expenditure from endowments. In Colombia the National University in 1962 derived over 90 per cent of its income from the national treasury and the rest from student fees. The departmental universities had three sources of income: nearly half was derived from the national exchequer and about a third from local budgets, leaving the rest to be earned from fees. Nearly 80 per cent of the income of the private universities had to be obtained from student fees, and the rest, apart from small contributions from local authorities, came from the State (*Asociación Colombiana de Universidades*, 1965). In some countries tuition is free in the state colleges but rarely so in the private institutions. In others, fees are payable everywhere, but are always higher in the private universities. For development and equipment the private institutions depend considerably on foundations such as Ford, Rockefeller and Kellog, but to match the international contributions some have raised large sums from previously untapped sources: in recent years, for example, the Technological University of Monterrey in Mexico has received generous contributions from local enterprises. It may be anticipated that as expenditure increases with the expansion of the university sector, the public contribution will grow, and the danger either of the dead hand of officialdom or of political interference will be intensified. Colombia has found a safeguard against this in the National University Fund which operates within the framework of the National Association of Universities. The Fund bears some resemblance to the British University Grants Committee and distributes the national grants to university funds. Since it comes under the general supervision of the National Congress of Universities and has access to the extensive knowledge of university development and of the problems of individual members, which has been accumulated by the parent association, its decisions are both soundly based and free from political influence.

Student participation in university affairs

To return to the third theme of the Manifesto of Cordoba, the demand for greater student participation in the running of the university was the most provocative of the claims put forward and has proved the most disturbing, at any rate to academic life. Students, organized and unorganized, have from time to time made decisive interventions in the process of university development, and pretend to a revolutionary role in the striving for national social and economic change. An evaluation of this contribution will be made in the second part of this volume, but at this point a brief summary of the course of events will suffice. In Argentina and Uruguay, where the movement had its origin, the students obtained their objectives fully in official universities. In Uruguay, although there were set-backs in the time of dictatorship, the Law of 1958 confirmed co-government and gave the students twenty seats, and the alumni twenty seats in the General Assembly of the University, as against thirty to the teaching staff, and a similar pattern of representation on the other organs of university government. The students could muster twenty votes towards the majority of forty-six votes out of seventy required for the election of the Rector, and ten towards the majority of twenty-four votes out of thirty-five for the election of a dean (Pelaez, 1963). On the other side of the Andes in Chile they did not achieve effective representation, and very little in Brazil, and that only latterly. They did somewhat better in Peru, Bolivia and Venezuela, but in Colombia they achieved no influence on the Council, though they are represented in the *Consiliatura*. In Honduras the students control 50 per cent of the seats in the governing councils. Student representation on the organs of the private universities is not common.

It is not, unfortunately, solely through constitutional channels that Latin American students choose to make their voice heard. Courses are at times interrupted by strikes and demonstrations or by an almost insolent disregard for the rights of others. Nor are these manifestations confined to internal university matters. It is considered a matter of right and pride for the student to intervene in national politics, making of the university campus a platform for all kinds of causes which have little to do with academic matters, a privileged platform too, as university autonomy is interpreted to mean that the civil forces of the law and the armed forces have no right of access to the campus. Recently, for example, in 1965 in Colombia this claim to create disorder with immunity was even held to be valid beyond the precincts of the university in the streets of the city. In the past the private universities and particularly the religious foundations have been free from student troubles, partly because they have avoided the unfavourable situations which arise from part-time staff and political appointments. Discipline in private universities has been better; a healthy spirit has been fostered, and the authorities have at the same time never conceded the students' right to run the university, or to take part in political activity on the campus. The fact that the majority of students come from middle-class homes with a strong religious background, and that they pay not inconsiderable fees may also curb any tendency towards political protest. Whether this will prove to be so in the future may be in some doubt. Recently at an international conference of catholic educators at Buga in Colombia an innocuous resolution dealing with the desirability of more responsible attitudes on the part of students was accepted. This resolution has been interpreted in ways which were probably not intended by at least some of the eminent churchmen who attended, and was held to legitimize the demonstrations which followed shortly afterwards in the Catholic University of Peru. In recent years there has also been unrest among catholic students in Valparaiso and in Santiago de Chile. In the last five years civil authorities have reacted firmly to evidence that students were behind urban terrorism and linked with rural guerrilla activity in Bolivia, Venezuela, Guatemala and Colombia. The governments of Argentina, Mexico, Brazil and Colombia have made a fresh attempt to master this problem. Shortly after taking office in 1966, for example, the Liberal President of Colombia Dr Carlos Lleras Restrepo, had the ringleaders of violent demon-strations which were made against him on the campus of the National University arrested and brought before the courts, where they were sentenced. The majority of Colombian students have not seriously challenged these stern measures, but elsewhere in Argen-tina and Brazil a punitive policy has been less successful, driving many teachers out of the universities.

Student enrolment

The university crisis has been aggravated by growing pressure on places caused by rising expectations and the increased output of the secondary schools. Some indication of this demand is given by the appearance of new universities in the current century and especially during the last two decades. Argentina, with twenty-one million people in 1961, had fifteen universities with seven more aspirants to university status. Colombia with a smaller population had twenty-five, the same as Mexico, without counting those that styled themselves universities but were not recognized. Brazil had two more, and even the smallest Latin American country had at least one. In the last seven years quite a number of new ones have opened their doors.

Enrolment of university students has increased during the last decade at the rate of almost 8 per cent per year. This was somewhat less than in the period 1950–5 when the rate was over 12 per cent per year, but it still represents substantial numbers of people. The increase was smaller in Argentina and Chile with relatively well-developed systems of higher education, and higher in the north of the continent. In Colombia between 1959 and 1964 the yearly rate of increase was 11·49 per cent for first year students, and 13·46 per cent for all students. During this period the total number of students rose from 20,534 to 38,558, of which something over half were in public universities. The Association of Universities estimated that allowing for wastage there would be more than 80,000 students in higher education in 1968, of whom 25,000 would be in their first year, and ICETEX has calculated that by 1975 over a hundred thousand students would be studying at universities, but that even with this total the production of graduates would fall short of the country's needs by some thirty-four thousand (ICETEX, 1966).

In spite of improved enrolment the majority of the republics have a bottom-heavy educational structure, with the mass of young people receiving the minimum of schooling and an extemely small proportion graduating from university. In 1961 Argentina was a long way ahead of the others with ninety-three students in institutions of higher education for every ten thousand of the population, less than half the United States figure. Next came Uruguay with forty-eight, and then Cuba and Chile in the upper thirties. Ecuador, Peru, Colombia, Venezuela, Costa Rica and Mexico formed a group with around thirty students per ten thousand. Brazil had fourteen, and below her came the Central American Republics, but excluding Costa Rica. The situation was in fact somewhat less favourable than the ratios would indicate. An undesirably high proportion of the students enrolled in some countries were in the first year. Selection was often almost non-existent outside Argentina, Brazil and Chile. The secondary leaving certificate, the *bachillerato*, was usually adequate to gain a place, though it was not necessarily evidence of the applicant's ability to undertake work at university level. Some universities, for example those in Peru, set a separate entrance test and called also for certificates of good health and good conduct. The better universities by virtue of their reputation attract the most gifted candidates, but many institutions take whoever comes along, and usually their failure and wastage rates are high, of it they are not, the reason would lie in factors other than academic strictness. In Colombia between 1950 and 1963 the overall wastage rate approached 50 per cent, ranging from 13 per cent in theology and 18 per cent in law, to 67 per cent in philosophy and 72 per cent in civil engineering. In many cases the failure was related to economic difficulties, but inability to make the grade was the most important cause. In 1966 the National University of Colombia increased its enrolment by 50 per cent to twelve thousand students. In the Department of Chemistry 80 per cent of the record enrolment of freshmen failed to reach a satisfactory level in the terminal examination. It is much the same in other countries, and unfortunately especially in those with low enrolment ratios in higher education. Countries such as Argentina have a better record; their higher education systems are more stable and are based on a more mature secondary level.

Standards

Standards vary considerably from one university to another throughout Latin America, and indeed from one department to another within the same university. Low standards are the rule rather than the exception, and the reasons are not in dispute. In the first place the student arrives ill-prepared to begin academic specialization or to work on his own. Though the traditional function of the secondary schools has been to serve as a channel to the university, few of them succeed in installing the habit of reading. Most universities have a proportion of part-time students following evening courses, and some are no more than evening institutes whose facilities are used by young people already tired after a day's work. Libraries are almost non-existent in some places.The universities of Argentina are well provided, Buenos Aires having half a million volumes and La Plata a quarter of a million. The national universities of Chile and Uruguay have half a million each. At the other end of the continent Monterrey, for example, has one hundred thousand volumes. In Colombia the Andes has a good central library and an adequate specialist library in economics. The National University has some excellent faculty libraries, including the library of the Faculty of Agriculture at Medellin which has an international repute. The book resources of some of the smaller universities, however, are pathetic. The Colombian Association of Universities calculated in 1964 that simply to cope with the need for books of additional students who would enter universities by 1968 two million volumes would have to be added to the libraries.

Some of the new universities have made special efforts to establish and maintain high standards. There has been no exact Latin American parallel to the arrangements in British territories whereby new colleges such as the University College of the West Indies in Jamaica, were constituted as parts of the University of London until they felt their standards were sufficiently established to warrant independent status as full universities offering their own degrees. Nevertheless, the special relationship which enabled the University of the Andes during the early years of its existence to send its engineering students to complete their degree course to the University of Illinois, and other North American universities, was not entirely different. The scheme helped 'the Andes' to build up reputable standards so that when later it came to complete its own degrees they were widely accepted. The Technological Institute of Monterrey in Mexico adopted a different and unique method in Latin America to attain the same end. It sought membership of the Southern Association of Colleges and Schools of the United States of America. The application committed the University to a profound self-examination of every aspect of the work, and subsequently to a prolonged investigation of its report by a visiting inspection team on the part of the Association. Membership was only granted when the Association had satisfied itself that the standards of the University of Monterrey were of the highest.

University staff

Perhaps the most urgent problem facing universities is that of building up an adequate body of qualified staff. The recruitment of teachers has not kept pace with student enrolment. The Association of Colombian Universities has recorded that between 1957 and 1964 the number of full-time teachers in universities rose by one thousand, but in the face of the massive increase in student numbers the ratio students–full-time teacher deteriorated from 20·5 to 20·8, and to maintain the ratio at that level it would be necessary to recruit 1,840 additional staff by 1968. Many universities depend excessively on part-time teachers. It is becoming increasingly recognized in advanced countries that there is benefit to both sides in an eminent industrialist or medical specialist giving some of his time to academic work, and vice versa, and certainly in South America there are men of high professional repute who are serving in a double role. Too often, however, teachers are working part-time in Latin America from sheer economic necessity. Though university teaching is everywhere a cut above school-teaching, salaries are not princely, especially in private foundations, and not infrequently the national treasury may be months in arrears in providing the money. Two jobs may be complementary: an office in town which may provide most of the income, and a post at the university which does no harm to one's reputation. This usually means that there is no time for research, no time for student counselling or tutorials, and none to devote to the running of the department or to the life of the university. Even teaching is just a chore to be performed in a desultory fashion, or, if business is pressing, perhaps neglected altogether. Since at the same time, at any rate in the less developed countries, senior appointments are not rarely made on political grounds, the heads of departments changing with each party wind, university teaching sometimes lacks purpose, continuity and indeed everything that would normally be thought essential for high standards.

At this stage no altogether favourable comment could be made on the state of university development in Latin America. Standards of research and of teaching leave a good deal to be desired. Examples of university contribution to economic and social development seem few. In spite of growth in enrolment, the university still appears to be the preserve of a small privileged section of the community, which is unwilling, or at least lacks the will, to introduce change. Even now nearly 80 per cent of the students at the University of São Paulo could be classified as upper or upper-middle class; 56 per cent in the University of Buenos Aires, and 40 per cent in San Marcus in Lima, and all but a small proportion of the rest would be covered by the term lower-middle class (Howard W. Burns, 1963). Some observers would attribute the small element of students of working-class origin to the machinations of oligarchies. This interpretation is no doubt too sweeping, bearing in mind that in some Western countries the working-class child has to be both gifted and determined to survive through to the university. Nevertheless, the achievement is very far behind the example of North America, and less than the anticipations of the nineteen-eighteen reformists.

In spite of legitimate criticism, South American has none the less its eminent universities and research institutes, and its share of Nobel prize winners. The striving for excellence has not been abandoned. All over the continent universities private and official have development plans all of which make provision for improvement in the standards of teaching. The University of the Andes, Bogotá, for example, has been arranging facilities for brilliant students to seek high academic qualifications abroad with a view to teaching in the university. At the same time from the Faculty of Economics alone it has been sending an average of four lecturers a year overseas to obtain higher degrees. A similar scheme operates in the Technical University of Monterrey in Mexico and in other universities. One of the priorities of the national plan of the Colombian Association of Universities is the improvement of university teaching. The suggestion is made that the activities of individual universities in arranging postgraduate courses abroad for their staff should be supplemented by the establishment of an Interuniversity Graduate College, which would offer courses leading to specialist qualifications, a sort of *agrégation* for university teachers, as well as short refresher courses and seminars. It was calculated that the cost of producing a university teacher in such a college would be less than in the United States, $3,000 as compared with $4,000 a year. The idea of a college offering facilities for research and the training of university staff has gained currency beyond national boundaries in the concept, originally formulated by Bolivia, of a graduate College of the Americas.

PART TWO

Part Two is a survey of some factors and pressures
bearing on educational policies.

6

The forming of opinion and the role
of education

The past has contributed to the inequality of educational opportunity between the social classes, between different racial groups, and between town- and country-dwellers. At the same time there have always been factors which made for cohesion, notably the Spanish and Portuguese languages, the general acceptance of Roman law and the Roman Catholic faith. In recent years these traditional elements of Latin American civilization have been reinforced by new influences which have made the peoples of the continent think more in common terms, and also have stirred the deeply engrained attitude of passive acceptance of poverty and injustice. New channels of argument and appeal have been created. Even the violence, which has been long characteristic, is now being interpreted almost everywhere as an ultimatum to the privileged, and has convinced many people of conscience of the need to relieve the social injustice which weighs on the poor. Very few now question the importance of improving the provision of education in order to remove the barriers which confined the peon to his station, even though each country may be discovering its own difficulties in implementing the new-found ideal. It is the object of this second section to consider some of the factors which are stimulating new thinking about education in Latin America, and equally those which are prompting arguments about the role of education in development, and about the pace of social and educational reform.

The impact of technology

The advent of technology has been the main leavening agent. It has revealed the extent of the isolation of many communities and has begun the process of bringing the parts closer together. In the days when the pack mules took a week to make the journey from Guaya-quil to Quito even a small country like Ecuador was severed into two, the coastlands and the high mountains, each having its own ways and loyalties. In a country the size of Brazil the extremities were continents apart. First the railroad, and more recently the motor road and the air have made communication between the cities and provinces easier, carrying them all in some degree towards a common technological way of life. In Colombia air services link every city and town of any size. The airports are not unlike bus stations in the regularity of their services between provincial centres, and with the introduction of jet flights it is possible to reach the farthest points of the country in an hour. Most parts of Brazil may be reached by frequent air services, and a journey from Rio Grande to Manaous or from Recife to the upper Amazon now takes only some six hours by jet. The transport systems of Argentina and Mexico are reasonably well developed and only in Honduras and Guatemala are communications still unsatisfactory. The Latin American countries have also begun to develop a co-ordinated approach towards transportation. The Latin American Association of Ship-owners, shortly after its inauguration in 1964, made a General Agreement on Sea, River and Lake Transport which looked forward to members acting together for their mutual interest. About the same time a Latin American Railways Association was formed to press for a common rail policy, and particularly for the adoption of a uniform gauge throughout the continent.

The development of communications has overcome the obstacle of sheer size and encouraged the promotion of internal economic links, a development which was not attractive when each country was concerned with simply exporting its own particular primary product to Europe and North America in return for manufactured goods. It was this sort of thinking which led to the creation of the Latin American Free Trade Area. The Montevideo Treaty, by which LAFTA was founded in 1960 called upon all member countries to eliminate existing tariffs on trade among themselves within a twelve-year period, and recognized the importance of co-ordinated industrial development. Although LAFTA has not made the progress looked for, largely because industrial development in the member countries has not been complementary, the members of the Central American Common Market, also established in 1960, have already virtually achieved the elimination of tariffs between them, and have gone a good way towards harmonizing tax systems and monetary policies. This regional grouping has paved the way to two others. In 1966 Chile, Colombia, Venezuela, Ecuador and Peru signed the Declaration of Bogotá, by which they set themselves specific steps towards integration, more practical because more limited than those encouraged by LAFTA. The other regional group within the Free Trade Area includes Argentina, Bolivia, Brazil, Paraguay and Uruguay, all of which have an interest in the integrated development of the River Plate basin.

It is not simply technology alone which is marshalling the countries of Latin America along the same track. No less than other underdeveloped regions the continent is under the unrelenting pressure of the rise in the numbers of mouths it has to feed. With the improvement of medical services, and particularly with the eradication of malaria, coupled with the high birth-rate characteristic of countries which are predominantly Roman Catholic, the population of Colombia leaped from eleven and a half millions in 1951 to almost seventeen and a half in 1966, and will probably have doubled itself within twenty-five years. Colombia's rate of population increase at 3·2 per cent is one of the highest in South America. Only Venezuela and Brazil with 3·4 per cent are higher. Argentina has a rate of 1·8 per cent, and another comparatively advanced country, Uruguay, shares with a country of high infant mortality, Bolivia, the lowest rate of 1·4 per cent.

To planners everywhere the high birth-rate points to a large future labour force, but with half the population of the continent below the age of fifteen years it also means a greater number of unproductive children who have to be educated in some way and have to be fed in the meantime. It is the population explosion on top of the eruption of violence which has brought home to many South Americans the necessity to work out solutions together to improve the level of production. Some pioneers have begun an effort to change deeply entrenched attitudes to birth control. The International Planned Parenthood Federation has committed the largest part of its 1968 budget to activities in Latin America. Special efforts are being made to bring doctors from all over the continent for special training in Chile; the Western Hemisphere Regional Council will meet in Bogotá; and in Mexico family planning is to be added to the curriculum of medical schools. For the moment the mass of people remain unresponsive to this message. The informed at least may accept that an economic revolution brings with it inescapably a social revolution; a modern economy can be achieved only when the social disparities, ignorance and squalor which are legacies of the past, are eliminated. Very few think as yet in terms of limiting the number of new mouths to be fed.

All this does not indicate that the isolation and disparities of the past have been overcome. The average citizen of the South American republics boasts still the limited horizons of patriotism, and is ready to point out that the outsider is not always sufficiently sensitive to appreciate the barriers which separate each country. And even within a few minutes car or plane journey from the thriving modern conurbations the unproductive jungle and mountain still exist. Great extremes of wealth and poverty are still accepted by many as inevitable. However, technology is removing the barriers and, more significant than the simple fact of doing so, education for a technological age is offering promise of escape from poverty which is rousing the whole continent. In the ten years since Lucio Costa, the Brazilian town-planner, won the competition with his design for a new capital, Oscar Niemeyer and his associate architects have produced a city which has been admired the world over. Brasilia has brought the whole of that enormous country together. Every part of the nation has contributed something of its manners and customs. It is, however, more than an example of the unifying impetus of technology. Though it already has its slums and may not have developed the fullness of life which a mature community has, and lacks the variety of intellectual activity, fashion, entertainment that the sophisticated seek in a capital city, far more dramatically than the new town in Britain, it stands for the possibility of a life less poor and brutish, which modern technolgical education now offers to the dispossessed. In advanced industrial societies, the new technical discovery, however remarkable, is part of a slow growth which is not exciting. In Latin America, though there are frequently reasons for cynicism, the imagination of the visionaries and equally of the masses has been seized by the promise of new wealth to be created by the engineer and the architect. Oil has brought fabulous riches to Venezuela and raised her *per capita* income to the highest level in South America. Not enough of this has gone into building schools or into raising the productivity of the rural areas, this is admitted, but some has been invested in one of those spectacular industrial complexes which increasingly encourage great hopes of future prosperity. The area south-east of the Orinoco towards the borders of Guyana is rich in hydro-electric power, iron ore and petroleum. The Orinoco provides good communications to the sea and at the same time, with reclamation, the rich alluvial soil of the delta can provide the basis for cattle-raising and diverse agriculture. In the midst of this region a new city, Ciudad Guyana, has arisen as the centre of a huge planned industrial enterprise with steel mills, aluminium smelting, timber and pulp industries. It has already reached a population of one hundred thousand, which is expected to treble within five years as the pattern of industrial activity grows and becomes more variegated. Even government supporters may speak of the enterprise as a folly, to be compared with the empty Hotel Humboldt, perched by the egotistic whim of the dictator General Pérez Jiménez on Mount Avila 4,000 feet above Caracas. For many it is rather an act of faith, which is confidently expected to make the wilderness of trees produce the means for a better life for Venezuelans, and a safeguard against the time when the precious store of oil is exhausted. The Concepción area of Chile offers another more advanced example of planned industrial pioneering as part of a national concept of economic growth. The integrated steel plant at Huachipato, planned under the aegis of the Chilean Development Corporation, after nearly twenty years operation has now reached an annual capacity of half a million tons, and is the core of a complex of integrated industrial development. The present achievement is only the beginning of the upfolding of regional growth and there are further schemes on the stocks, and the promise of better living standards is already becoming a reality. Though they may be open to much criticism, projects such as Cuidad Guyana and Huachipato have a tremendous impact on the minds of people, releasing new aspirations and particularly underlining the urgent necessity for overhauling the systems of education. The examples carry the more weight because both are away from the capital cities, one in remote and backward territory. They counterbalance the overwhelming monopoly of ability and resources which everywhere the capitals have imposed on outlying areas, and offer the underdeveloped provinces the prospect of emulating the standards of the metropolis. They prompt increasingly pressing demands for modernization of the rural sector.

Urban life

It is not, however, only the expectation of material improvement excited by the exceptional showpieces of technological development which is noteworthy. Industry is growing everywhere, and in the new industrial areas new attitudes are evolving. Urban growth has been a factor making for uniformity of outlook, in spite of the distinctions between different social and economic levels. And the concentration of people in towns has brought more to share a common urban way of life which is becoming characteristic not only of the continent but of the world. Around the old towns new industrial suburbs are springing up, drawing in peasants from the surrounding countryside, creating urgent needs for training and reorientation, setting unprecedented standards of urban housing and living, and bringing into existence communities with interests and aspirations formerly unknown. When, two or three decades ago, the textile industries of Medellin in Colombia began to grow, to attract the Antioqueñian peasant, the industrialists built houses more modern and better serviced than those common in rural areas, and so set a level of social expectations for the future. At the same time the limited facilities of the factories themselves for training the unskilled country labour had to be supplemented by schools for elementary and vocational education supplied by the community, since an industrial society could not be built with a largely illiterate and unskilled working force. The sole sources of work ceased to be the rural landowner, and the wealthy official or merchant of the town. The factories absorbed the farm labourers, and even more particularly the domestic servants, who for centuries had enabled the almost feudal style of life in the large houses to be maintained. Even now at least one *muchacha* is found in the most humble household claiming to be middle class, but to many more the factories offer an alternative to household service, and an escape from submission to the style of thinking of their 'betters'. Those who formerly voted as they were expected, or if they were female did not vote at all, are influenced increasingly at the ballot box as much by what they hear

96

on the workshop floor as from the pulpit. Though there are many factory workers who lack knowledge and understanding of the issues involved, organized union activity is growing, and even if unions may not yet have developed an independent viewpoint and emancipated themselves from external influences to the extent that has been achieved in Argentina, for example, they serve to formulate the social aspirations of their members, and they add a voice to the insistent demand for educational opportunity. While some old families are slipping down the economic scale new groups are eroding traditional influence (Fals Borda, 1961). A new élite of lawyers, accountants and managers are appropriating decision-making roles in the expanding industrial society. They have a clear stake in development, are severely critical of the privileged minorities who belong to the past, and are intensely ambitious for their children, demanding for them educational opportunities which they themselves may have enjoyed only at great sacrifice. In the towns the traditional ways of thinking and long-accepted conventions are giving way before new influences. Aspiration and resentment are present in the new suburbs, and both are working for change.

The spirit of revolt

In Peru, Colombia and Venezuela particularly industrialization may have absorbed a disproportionate part of available resources. It is said that the countryside has been sacrificed in the interests of industrial expansion and that the shortcomings of policy have combined with the weakness of the infrastructure, and the poor price of coffee, sugar and bananas on the world market in keeping the country areas backward. It is not fortuitous that in spite of the conservatism of the peasant rural resentment has smouldered into open violence in Peru, Colombia and Venezuela, and that in the latter two countries it has not proved possible to prevent guerrillas with Cuban support disturbing the writ of the Government over wide areas. On 15 February 1966, together with four companions the former Roman Catholic priest Camilo Torres was shot dead when the guerrilla band, which he had joined four months before, attempted to ambush an army patrol in the Colombian province of Santander. His death made a profound impression on catholics, politicians, students, workers and peasants in Colombia and beyond, for in his short and restless life he brought together all the conflicts and pressures of his time. He was born in 1929 of a respected middle-class family. His father was a medical doctor, former university teacher and rector of the National University. He completed his secondary studies in Bogotá in 1947 and entered the law school of the National University. After a few months, against the wishes of his family, he abandoned law to enter the *Seminario Conciliar* in Bogotá. His evident interest in social problems and outstanding intellectual ability prompted the Church authorities to send him after his ordination in 1954 to study sociology at the Belgian Catholic University of Louvain, where he remained six years. When he returned to Bogotá he was appointed chaplain of the National University and Professor of Sociology. Already were formed in his mind ideas which, though they exhilarated the student generation, were to disturb the Church and shock his own class, and ultimately to lead to his death. To him a revolutionary change of ideas, or as he would have chosen to put it a revolutionary return to Christian ideals, had to come about if the terrible social injustices suffered by the mass of the people were to be eliminated against the obstinacy of the ruling minorities, and even at this stage of the development of his thought, violence may have seemed an inevitable part of the process of social change. Camilo Torres aligned himself unreservedly with the students in demonstrations of protest against the established order, whether academic or civic. The students, his ardent adherents, were flattered by the role he attributed to them in the evolution of social justice. Students were unique agents of change because in them two qualities, not to be found elsewhere in Latin America, were combined, a high level of culture and intelligence together with an unbridled disrespect for the establishment. Faced with his revolutionary political inclinations, which became clearer each day, the Church hierarchy took alarm and invited him to lay down his functions at the university, to take up a post in the Centre for Social Research, where it was thought he could do no harm. Later he gave the impression that the withdrawal from the university did not worry him. In November 1965 he was to write in a message to students that their contribution to the cause of revolution was transitory and superficial because they were not committed economically or in any way to the struggle. When the student obtained his degree he ceased to be a rebel, and diverted his energies to making a place for himself in the society which he formerly rejected (Guzman, 1967). This is a true enough comment on the reformist impact of students, and suggests one explanation why half a century of the university reform movement had not resulted in more fundamental changes in Latin American society. It is, however, worth making a short digression to point out that the remarks were apt only in a general way. The majority of students, if they take part in demonstrations at all, do so out of youthful high spirits rather than fierce political convictions, but they do not give the whole picture. Student movements also contain small groups of determined individuals, whether agents infiltrated or genuine students, who use the organizations to propagate ideas which are certainly dangerous to the established order; and when the occasion requires, translate the ideas into action. From 1917 onwards student unions have made their presence felt on numerous occasions of political crisis. Students played a significant role in the Cuban revolution and the example is being enthusiastically followed. Recently it was reported from La Paz that a woman student of philosophy was one of the principal links between the Che Guevara operating in the south-east of Bolivia and the capital and that there was talk of a student–miner anti-government pact. The establishment of the Continental Latin American Students' Organization in Havana in 1966 was a clear indication that more activity of this kind was planned. Governments are not unconvinced about the seriousness of the students' efforts to influence the course of development, and in some cases recently have reacted with firmness to restrict the students' freedom to intervene in the situation.

To return to the lost sheep of the Church, Camilo Torres now directed his attentions to the wider political world, and at first with the help of the opposition parties of the left, he published the periodical *Frente Unido*, and started to speak on platforms all over the country, each utterance becoming a more frantic appeal for action than the last. In the course of months his political commitment became intolerable to the Church, and after an uncompromising meeting with the Archbishop of Bogotá, he abandoned his priestly robes. By this time his revolutionary Christianity and his insistence on appealing to the uncommitted exasperated his political allies. Their lukewarm support decided him to throw in his lot with the guerrillas in the mountains, and one evening of drizzling rain he left Bogotá by the road to the north and to his death.

Camilo Torres may well turn out to be of no interest to history, and indeed there seems no sign that his secret burial place, were it known, would become a place of pilgrimage as the Government feared. His death, nevertheless, prompted comment from many parts of Latin America. None of the obituaries were utterly critical, and the few which used expressions like *bandalero* were generally thought to be unjust. It is curious that his fate aroused sympathy from every sector of society. Even the Church could say, through the Press secretary of the Archbishop of Panama, that respect was due to a man who preferred the smear 'communist' to keeping silent in the face of a society insensitive to the Christian message of justice and charity. The political journals of the left spoke of his death as shaking the conscience of the nation, and while those of different complexion may have judged him mad, or naïve, or misguided, or deceived, they acknowledged that he had sacrificed his life for an ideal of social justice. Though without a following Camilo Torres epitomized the impatient aspirations of his generation. Within the Church he represented the search for *Neuva Cristiandad*, and in his links with political parties he marked the change of interest away from the intense lay-clerical conflicts of the past towards the over-riding need for social and economic advance. Through his work with students he stood for the idealism of the young against the older generation's defence of the status quo. His research as a sociologist into the problems of rural community development, cited in the third section of this book, equated the interests of the country with those of the town, and as a social reformer he championed the underprivileged in both town and country against the exploitation of the wealthy and the powerful. His personal influence will ultimately be small, but he embodied many of the forces which are shaping future patterns of society and the educational reforms on which they must be based.

Camilo Torres was the son of the Church generally thought of as a strong influence on the side of reaction. Certainly in Colombia the pulpit has been used to resist political doctrines which smacked of communism, even to the extent of guiding the flock in the way to vote. The great conflicts the Church conducted in the past against the anti-clericalism of the Liberals have left a legacy of unprogressive attitudes and a reputation for siding with the privileged minorities. Even though the Liberals and Conservatives are co-operating for the time being and old conflicts are stilled, the Church appears ever fearful of change. Members of the Congregation rein-force this impression by hiding behind the protection of the Church in order to maintain backward-looking habits of thought. Catholic parents have not shrunk from invoking the Church to harass per-haps some unfortunate teacher unwary enough to introduce pro-gressive ideas to his class. Yet there is also in the Roman Catholic Church in South America a movement for social reform, evidenced not only by Camilo Torres but also by the radio schools movement, the *Universidad Obrera* at Cali, and by Christian democratic move-ments in other parts of the continent.

At the southern end of the Andes another priest trained at Louvain is Professor of Sociology at the Catholic University of Chile and an active research worker into social problems. As a social reformer Father Roger Vekeman has found ready ears in the ruling party, the Christian Democratic Party. When Eduardo Frei carried the Christian Democrats to power in 1964 with 54 per cent of the votes his victory was hailed as the alternative to the Cuban way to reform. Indeed, there was something revolutionary in the election success as it was achieved without any of the normal arrange-ments with other parties, either with the socialist–communist Popular Action Front, FRAP, or with the Radicals, who felt their place had been usurped. The Conservative National Party saw in the new government's policies dangerous interference with the natural unfolding of the social and economic process, and with the traditional role of the great landowners of maintaining the stability of the state. The opposition succeeded in holding up the passing of the Agrarian Reform Bill, a vital part of the Government's programme of rural development, for two years until the presidential party ultimately won a majority in Congress in 1967. Eduardo Frei, born of a middle-class Swiss immigrant family, entered the Catholic University of Santiago already a passionate social reformer. He was the founder of the reformist *Falange Nacional*, which shortly changed its name to *Partido Demócrata Cristiano*, the first of the Christian democratic parties to spread over the whole of Latin America. It was a party of democratic reform whose programme contained three interdependent elements; education, industry and agriculture. Education was the key to the other two, but reform of education without the others would result simply in frustration. Progress in both town and country must depend on the slow progress of human development. A policy of gradualness does not satisfy all and is difficult to maintain in the face of setbacks. The moderates in the PDC are having difficulty in holding ground against those who feel that some co-operation with FRAP would lead to more rapid progress.

Venezuela similarly embarked on an experiment in reform when the dictator Pérez Jiménez was overthrown in 1958 by the combined action of political parties and students, and *Acción Democrática* took over the direction of affairs. In 1963, when Raul Leoni succeeded his party colleague Rómulo Betancourt in the presidency, Venezuela experienced a peaceful change of government by the process of election for the first time in its history. Yet in spite of a decade of peaceful development backed by the revenues from oil, many Venezuelans feel themselves to be forgotten amidst the prosperity. Only now is *Acción Democrática* turning its attention to the shocking contrast between the elegant villas and skyscrapers of Caracas and the miserable hovels which girdle the city with envy. The Party's relative neglect of the building of schools and the development of agriculture has provoked discontent, and the university students, once powerful supporters, have become bitter critics of the Government's record. The students are suspected of maintaining links with Castro, who, it is claimed, is attempting to disturb the stability of the country by means of political murder in the cities and guerrilla activity in the mountains. While pursuing a firm policy against subversion, the ruling party is making efforts to improve its appeal to the less privileged sections of the population, because it is clear that if social progress cannot be clearly shown in motion, discontent with the flaunting of riches and the arrogance of the fortunate could bring wide acceptance of the message of the bearded Cuban leader.

Revolutionary change

The Venezuelan Government does well to take the threat of Cuba seriously, for the island offers an example of another kind of solution to the evils of the time. The Cuban revolution claimed to have overthrown the traditional social structures as a starting-point for economic and technological reform. Central to the castroite creed is the principle that the broadening of educational opportunity can be achieved only after the social debris of the past has been cleared away. Whether the claim is valid or not, *fidelismo* still exercises a powerful influence over the impatient throughout Latin America, to the detriment of the standing of the Mexican model. Students were not involved in the Mexican struggles, and though Che Guevara is not known for his achievements in the educational field he is more familiar to the younger generation throughout Latin America than any Mexican revolutionary hero. Yet the earlier upheaval did lead to fundamental changes in the role of education in Mexican society. The Mexican revolution followed a path familiar enough, a patriotic 'government', set up in a provincial city after a period of maladministration and instability, attracting support away from the existing government in the capital, the typical *pronunciamiento*. In the past a revolutionary *golpe* would still the conflicting voices only for a time, after which the interests of town and country, conservatives and progressives would clash again. The Mexican revolution created a unique way to silence the contradictory voices – a single official party, *Partido Revolucionario Institutional*, PRI, which incorporates three organizations, the *Confederación de Trabajadores Mexicanos* CTM, for labour, the *Confederación Nacional de Campesinos*, CNC, for peasants, and the *Confederación Nacional de Organizaciones Populares*, CNOP, for intellectuals, civil servants and army personnel. These new organs have led to a peaceful and corporate effort of the whole nation to achieve its aspirations through a social order in which material benefits are enjoyed not only by a privileged minority but also are shared by all sections of the nation, and by the country as much as by the town. Rural electrification and irrigation of the northern deserts as well as the successful development of industry are among the achievements of the Mexican revolution. Education has also been at the head of the nation's priorities, and massive literacy campaigns, the expansion of technological education, and the creation of the huge campus of the University of Mexico have contributed to growth. After nearly fifty years of unsensational progress, however, though Mexico's stock wins an increasingly solid reputation, and her artistic production stirs the imagination of her neighbours, the revolution has given way to Cuba's in the degree of ardour which it generates. To many it has become respectable and its methods are admired by those who hope that its achievements can be imitated without necessarily suffering the bloodshed and violence. It appears as a peaceful process of development which would not have required revolution at all if the government of Diaz had not been so especially bad. Nevertheless, the Mexican experiment was truly revolutionary in that it put aside the traditional interests of the privileged minorities in the name of the social progress of the whole nation. But if rural prosperity and the raising of the cultural level of the people have fallen short of the earlier high hopes, the image of the Cuban revolution is also not untarnished.

The debate continues

The choice is still open between the two alternatives pressing their claim to be the way ahead for Latin America. The Venezuelan–Chilean is the slow way, moving forward step by step on several fronts at the same time, material advances keeping pace with the gradual process of education and the evolution of ideas. *Fidelismo* offers the instant new world, to be built by a massive re-education programme after the outmoded privileges of the past have been swept away. In both education is crucial.

Between the countries which have chosen opposite solutions lie the uncommitted, or those countries in which the normal democratic process has not thrown up politicians able to maintain stable and progressive government. In Colombia, Peru, Ecuador, Bolivia, Paraguay, Brazil and even Argentina, the modern world of technology is challenging traditional modes of thought and organization without yet producing broadly accepted political solutions which might ease the strains.

In Colombia public discussion of education and its role in development takes place, but effective translation of ideas into action has been atrophied in large measure during the period of the *Frente Nacional,* The National Front to which the Conservatives and Liberals had recourse ten years ago in the hope that sinking the traditional conflict between the two parties would bring the violence to an end. By the terms of the agreement the two factions were to collaborate in running the country for fifteen years, each in turn providing the joint candidate for the presidency, and each taking half share of the seats in Congress and of public offices. Since any measure to be passed by Congress required a two-thirds majority nothing in any way controversial could have any chance of acceptance, and in any case such was the reaction to the horrors of the *violencia*, which had started as a clash between the two parties, that anything suggesting conflict was shunned, lest it gave rise to further bloodshed. The President between 1966 and 1970 is Dr Carlos Lleras Restrepo, of the Liberal Party, which is the more popular and better organized. Up to the present his government has been preoccupied with economic problems, which it has dealt with not unsuccessfully and to the satisfaction of the middle classes, convincing the restless that social and economic reform were under way. He has dealt firmly with student unruliness, but also plans temporarily to abolish the two-thirds voting rule, an action which would lead to more lively discussion in Congress and the country. It may be that the suspension of political controversy is coming to an end, but in the meantime Colombia remains in that group of countries which are attempting economic growth and technological innovation with the minimum of disturbance of existing social structures, together with Peru, and the republics under military régimes.

The military governments of Argentina and Brazil, whose problems are aggravated by their size, tend, so to speak, to the honest soldier's view that economic progress is both desirable and essential, and that, if possible, its benefits should be enjoyed by all sections of the population, but without disturbing the social order or public peace. Over much of Latin America one hundred and fifty years of independence have not been sufficient for durable democratic institutions to grow. The diversity in physical features and in peoples and cultures results in a fragmentation of interest and opinion which hitherto has not permitted the emergence of political parties with broadly based support. The armed forces, the instruments with which independence was won, subsequently claimed to be the guardians of the constitution, and many times in political and economic crises have intervened to prevent threats to the integrity of the republic. Even in Argentina the 'political cultural level' has not reached the heights attained in the economic sector and the relative feebleness of the civil institutions has led to repeated intervention by the military. Since 1930 there have been two periods of indirect military rule, the decade of Peronism when power rested on the armed forces in alliance with organized labour, and four direct military régimes, including the government of General Juan Orlos Organia, who came to power in 1966. General Organia appointed Dr Adalbert Krieger Vesena Minister of Economic Affairs to find a way out of an economic mess. The policy involved a 40 per cent devaluation, together with a massive cut in protective import duties and the introduction of new taxes to increase revenue. The problems of inflation and the modernization of the public services left little time for educational reform.

In Bolivia General Barrientos had the outbreak of guerrilla activity to compound the perennial problem of the discontent of the miners, and his concern with education has been limited to preventing collusion between the high school and university students and the guerillas and miners. The Brazilian military government's constitution of 1967 took some powers away from the provinces on the grounds that only forceful central control could overcome the problems of sheer size and economics, and while it did not interfere directly with the 1962 Education Act, it did not reinforce the decentralizing trend of that measure. Uruguay's government is not military in the normal sense, but General Oscar Gestido was elected to put some purpose into the task of restoring order and solvency after a period of economic stagnation, strikes and financial collapse. The problems of modernization of the stockbreeding industry, the halting of depopulation of the countryside, and the development of the first resources, have taken precedence over educational problems. Paraguay's General Stroessner had himself elected in 1954. Imposing order with a firm hand he carried out major projects of improvement in communications, and a programme of agrarian reform, without giving any special attention to education.

The common view that the military régimes are always reactionary, acting solely in the interests of the privileged classes and the Church, cannot be substantiated. In Argentina military rule has supported at different times the landowners, the radical middle classes and organized labour, while in Colombia General Rojas Pinilla's régime prior to the *violencia* was at loggerheads with the Church. The military is not so much the ally of any particular party or class, but an autonomous institution in its own right, which feels entirely justified in entering into the management of public affairs when the state and particularly its own functions are threatened. In recent years the armed challenge of Castro-inspired guerrillas has pushed the armed forces to the right of politics, or at any rate into a clearly anti-Cuba position (Finer, 1967). However, it is questionable whether the achievements of these régimes will prove so satisfying to all sections of the population as to isolate the countries from the fascination of *fidelismo*, or even from the opposing arguments which emanate from Chile and Venezeula on the one hand and Cuba and Mexico on the other. For the most part the military régimes are content to go along with the generalities of the inter-American conferences on matters of educational policy, even if in practice educational advance may be held up by economic crises. Public discussion about education is more or less in suspense, though particularly in Bolivia the students keep the subject before the attention of the nation.

The influence of the teaching profession

Teachers as a body do not have very much influence on the formulation of educational and social policies. From time to time they are obliged to protest, sometimes vigorously and bitterly, against delay in payments of salaries, but in the less developed countries organized representation does not go far. Early in 1966 Colombian primary school teachers took part in a march in the capital to demonstrate against the Government's failure to pay salaries. The column, which included representatives from all over the republic, stretched for several miles, and the neatness of the turn-out and orderliness of behaviour deeply impressed all who witnessed the parade. The Ministry officials who received the delegation must have realized that they were in earnest, not only about salaries but about the ultimate role of the teachers' association in the development of of Colombian education. In the long run, however, the demonstration had no lasting effect because the professional organizations have not the power to impose their views. Teaching, unfortunately, is a profession which ranks low in public esteem. The primary teacher in some countries is given a station little above that of the labourer, and if the secondary master is regarded with slightly more respect he rarely finds the salary of one job sufficient to maintain a middle-class way of life. Even the university *profesor* often cannot keep up the status accorded to his post without supplementing his income by running a professional practice in town. Teachers are also poorly organized to press a point of view. There is considerable rivalry within the profession, the teachers at each of the three levels feeling that they belong to quite distinct fields of activity without common interests. And even within the secondary level in Brazil, for example, the teacher's status varies with his subject, the teacher of the optional subjects, such as English, coming pretty low down in the hierarchy. Naturally some jealousy exists. Teachers not only do not experience a common feeling among themselves but rarely are able to give their undivided loyalty to a particular school, through which they might exert influence. Frequently they teach in more than one institution to make ends meet, or even follow more than one calling. This is particularly the case in universities. Whereas the students are not uncommonly very active in public debate, outside the formal class and the limits of the subject of the course, most university teachers are out of touch with those whom they teach. Little contact takes place because the teacher is occupied elsewhere. One healthy element in the exchange of ideas is missing, and the maturer members of the university fail to help the formation of student opinion. Generally, teachers are all too frequently in the role of humble petitioners, too involved with seeking boons, from departmental authority, to aspire to influence over educational policy. There may be some signs of a growing professional consciousness. The Confederation of Latin-American Educators is a long-established body of national professional associations, dependent financially entirely on its members' dues. The sixth Conference in 1957, responding to the spirit of the time, revived a resolution originally accepted in 1943, stressing the importance of democratic principles in educational and social development. At all events, even if they still do not present an organized body of opinion, it is safe to assume that in those countries where social privileges and outstanding wealth are constant irritants, teachers align themselves with the opponents of the oligarchy.

International organizations

One of the major groups of agents seeking to sway minds in Latin America consists of the international organizations. In bringing the peoples of the region closer together, the revolution in transportation has revealed to them that they share many problems. It has made it possible for them to talk together, and to think about common objectives, and about co-operation to achieve them.

The Organization of American States, the OAS, or, in Spanish, the OEA, grew out of the International Union of American Republics which was established during the nineteenth century to collect commercial information. In 1910 the name was changed to the Union of American Republics, and again in Bogotá in 1948 a charter was adopted which gave the organization its present shape and objectives. Its purpose was to strengthen peace and security, to prevent difficulties between member states, and to provide for common action and co-operation in social, economic and cultural matters. The supreme authority of the Organization was vested in the Inter-American Conference, and the day to day conduct of affairs was in the hands of the Council of the Organization. The secretariat was provided by the Pan-American Union, which had been the commercial bureau of the original Union. Under the main organs were specialist committees. The Inter-American Economic and Social Council, CIES, acted as co-ordinator over a wide field and was frequently concerned with educational problems. The Inter-American Rural Education Centre at Rubio in Venezuela was originally founded as the Inter-American Rural Normal School by CIES.

As early as 1906 at the third Conference of the Inter-American Union, it was agreed to call for information on educational matters, and since then the interest in education has increased. The Committee for Cultural Action, with a permanent seat in Mexico, arranged educational exchanges on behalf of the OAS, and in 1957 in response to the increasing appreciation of the role of education in development, the Inter-American Cultural Council was created to survey exchange activities and also to promote the adoption of the basic educational programmes suited to the varying needs of the population groups of Latin America. The activities of this Council reinforced the meetings of the Ministers of Education of the Republics which have now been taking place for two decades. The OAS has responded to the growing interest in education, and at the same time has influenced the lines of educational development. The turning-point was in 1956 when the Organization in collaboration with Unesco arranged a Regional Conference of Latin American States on Free and Compulsory Education at Lima, Peru. The Conference recommended that in all Latin American states there should be six years' free and compulsory education. Arising out of the meetings a major project was set up by Unesco with the object of facilitating co-operation in the planning and implementation of the resolution. Since that date Unesco has actively intervened in the development of primary education through numerous seminars and conferences, the most recent dealing with the major project itself, though certainly not the last, in Buenos Aires in 1966. In 1957 it published a study of the primary school curricula by the eminent Brazilian educationist Dr Lourenço Filho. It has contributed to the training of teachers by the establishment of model normal schools for rural teachers in Colombia, Ecuador, Nicaragua and Honduras, by co-operating with the Inter-American Rural Education Centre in Venezuela, and by sponsoring special courses in the Universities of São Paulo and Santiago de Chile.

Immediately after the 1956 joint conference the Ministers of Education took up the themes of the discussions in their second ministerial meeting. This meeting dealt with the various aspects of a major programme of universal primary education, going into finance, the separate responsibilities of governments, communities and individuals, the means of overcoming the shortage of trained teachers, school construction programmes, fundamental education in rural areas and the problems of educational administration. Though no binding commitments were entered into, under the stimulus of international discussion the Ministers were able to see the objectives towards which they should work, and to declare their intent to undertake educational reform. Usually in step with Unesco, the OAS followed up the declared intentions throughout the next decade or so, constantly persuading members to evaluate progress, and advising on the practical implementations of educational policies.

In 1954–5 the OAS had arranged an international seminar on secondary education at Santiago de Chile, which had drawn attention to the three vital roles of secondary schools, to provide a general education suited to the modern world, to train citizens and to provide a vocational preparation for work or professional studies at a higher level. The Santiago Conference stressed the need for flexibility and for equality of opportunity in the secondary sector and underlined the links with the primary school on the one hand, and with universities on the other. It suggested that there should be two cycles; the first complete in itself providing a general education leading either to higher study in a second cycle, or out into the working world; the second more specialized, either academic leading to the university, or technical leading either to technological institutions, or to a vocational qualification as a teacher or 'technician' according to the course. Much of the first-cycle curriculum would be compulsory, though at this level as in the second cycle there should be the opportunity for adaptation to the wishes of the individual students and to the needs of the area. The guidelines laid down at Santiago were followed generally throughout Latin America.

This series of conferences in 1955–6 covered the whole field of child education and had a tremendous influence on thinking and action in the subsequent years. One of the immediate results was a seminar organized by the OAS in Washington in 1958 on *Planeamiento Integral de la Educación* which was attended by high officials of the member republics. The discussions ranged over the scope and methods of integral planning, administration, finance and the expansion of planning departments. Three years later at Punta del Este the idea was carried farther when the *Alianza para el Progreso* was launched with the object of harnessing all available forces for a great spurt forward. There was no formal organization. Though for a time a panel of experts was set up to advise on development schemes, it was always the intention that existing forms of organization should be used to achieve the objectives, the Alliance supplying the stimulus and idealism. A ten-year plan was drawn up and accepted as the level of achievement to be aimed at. In the following year the Santiago Conference formulated a set of proposals for the furtherance of the plan, and these were accepted by the third Inter-American Conference of Ministers of Education at Bogotá, in 1963. By now the international organizations were attempting to give a powerful impetus to progress. The Santiago Conference itself was a co-operate effort, Unesco, the Economic Commission for Latin America, CREFAL, the International Labour Organization, and the Food and Agricultural Organization being included among the sponsors, as well as the Organization of American States. There was no doubt about the side of the fence international influence came down on. The *Declaration of Santiago* recorded that the participating states ratified their decision to co-ordinate educational development and economic progress in order to achieve a more just distribution of national wealth, and to open educational opportunities equally to all sections of the population. They pledged themselves to make these hopes a reality without sacrifice of independence. The members of the Conference were fully aware of the crucial importance of their decisions for history. They realized that their deliberations would probably decide whether the three hundred millions who would inhabit Latin American in 1970 would enjoy a better standard of life and enjoy the fruits of technological progress, or whether they would remain in poverty. They realized equally that what they did would decide whether the ends could be achieved through existing democratic institutions, or not. Their voice was for peaceful organic growth, laying stress on the progressive decentralization of educational administration in order to involve local and regional authorities and communities in a great co-operative effort for human development.

International conferences were now, so to speak, in full flood. In 1961, for example, Unesco shared in ten international conferences in Latin America, in 1962 in nineteen, in 1963 in sixteen and in 1964 in twenty-one. Not all were concerned with policies and planning: some were specialist meetings dealing with the teaching of physics or some other science, with university teaching and research, or with the application of science and technology to development. Many, however, had their origin in the conferences of 1956. For example in 1966, when of the sixteen meetings held in Latin America four were concerned respectively with planning and organization of literacy programmes, investment in education, higher education and the Major Project on primary education.

La Educación

One of the channels of communication along which the ideas and results of these conferences passed was the publication *La Educación*, started by the Pan American Union in 1956. The first number was given over to reporting the 1955-6 conferences. Then followed a series of issues each devoted to a special topic such as fundamental education, the education of adults, technical education and rural education. Number 11 contained a report on the 1958 Seminar on Planning, and Number 12 a report on a conference on inter-American educational exchanges held in Costa Rica. The Santiago Conference of 1962 on Education and Economic Development was reported in Nos. 25-26. There have also been issues devoted to schoolbuilding, higher education, the single teacher school, the primary school and a recent one on the educational programme of the Organization of American States itself. In addition to this regular periodical, the OAS has issued a stream of studies on every aspect of Latin American education which has been the subject of discussion at conferences.

There is no doubt that the international organizations and the conferences they have sponsored have powerfully stimulated discussion about education's role in national development, and have been perhaps the decisive factor in setting governments off on a programme of educational reform. In his opening address to the Washington seminar in 1958 Dr Guillermo Nannetti hit the appropriate note in speaking of the sensation of being on the verge of a new historical era, of the release of new social forces as a result of the mastering of the forces of nature, and especially of the significance of international integration in the process of educational development. His words, a little high-sounding to the Anglo-Saxon ear, a little unreal even, are typical of the inter-American conferences of the last decade. The oratory reflects the extent to which ideas were stirring and spreading over the continent, and heralds the willingness of governments to try the policies recommended to them. And yet there have also been serious misgivings. The impatient who incline towards radical solutions are not alone in finding the achievement less than the promise, and in decrying the overwhelming North American influence and generosity. Some see in the activities of the Organization of American States and its organs, as well as in the Alliance for Progress instruments of yankee imperialism, and props to support the status quo. The charge has an element of truth in so far as the North American influence in the inter-American organizations has pushed hard the policy of gradual evolution, the Chilean as opposed to the Cuban way. It is also true that the mass of Latin Americans remain unconvinced about the ability of the United States to co-operate in solutions acceptable to Latin pride and national integrity. The manner in which education expands and contributes to development will clear when the undecided make their choice between the rival claims of Cuba and Chile. Over much of Latin America the argument is still unresolved.

PART THREE

The third part of this book is devoted to an evaluation of the contribution of education to development mainly in a specific country, Colombia. After a discussion of two aspects of the subject not dealt with in detail earlier, adult and community education, and the overseas aid programme, an attempt is made to strike an overall balance.

I

7

Adult education and community development

Without highly trained manpower the Latin American republics have no possibility of offering their peoples the hope of social and economic progress. At the same time without informed and forward-looking ordinary people the effort of the most dedicated leaders can achieve little. The dilemma is all the more acute because the two claims are competing for the same inadequate resources. Nearly five centuries after the first settlements of the continent illiteracy is still widespread. Honduras has as many as 80 per cent of the population unable to read and write, Bolivia 70 per cent, and even in the advanced Argentina and Uruguay almost a tenth of the people suffer the same handicap. Among the millions of Indians who speak no Spanish, such as the Quechua of the Peruvian Andes, literacy almost does not exist. No one disputes that a population lacking basic education is a drag-chain on economic progress, and the eradication of illiteracy now dominates the thinking of many educational planners. But the realization of the vital importance of this objective has not proved as yet all that much more efficacious than qualms of conscience in eliminating the problem. In 1944 the Mexican President Avila Camacho called upon all literate persons between the ages of sixteen and sixty to teach reading and writing to illiterates, and two years later the *Dirección General de Alfabetización y Educación Extrascolar* was established to administer a national campaign against illiteracy. Centres for literacy were set up, readers published. Forty-eight motorized teams equipped with projectors and record-players were constituted, with social workers, nurses, agricultural experts and teachers of rural trades. By 1951, when Unesco established the Fundamental Education Centre for Latin America, CREFAL, at Patzcuaro on Mexican territory, it was claimed that over two million people had learned to read and write. But, in fact, the success of the movement was far from complete. The half-literate population, who were expected to serve as instructors, did not possess the ability to teach reading and writing, nor did the learners have the will and patience to persevere in the task. Moreover, it was never possible to get ahead of the ever-advancing tide of population increase, so that after twenty years of effort the illiteracy percentage remained unaltered. In 1942 42 per cent of the population of Mexico were unable to read: in 1963 the figure was 43 per cent (Larrea, 1963). Similarly in Colombia, though the percentage is steadily falling, the actual number of illiterates is in fact rising. At the beginning of the century almost three million people, representing 63 per cent of the population, were illiterate. By 1951 the proportion had dropped to 42 per cent, but the number had increased to almost five million, and in 1961, when the proportion had been reduced to 37·5 per cent, there were over five million Colombians unfamiliar with the printed word. Above the level of basic education there are few examples in Latin America of the kind of adult education which offers mature people the opportunity to broaden their understanding of the world they live in, or to improve their ability to cope with professional problems. Adult education associations and university extra-mural activities are limited or even unknown. At both levels there appears to be no consumer demand, or to avoid a twentieth-century expression, the mass of the citizens of the Latin American republics have so long carried the burden of poverty and oppression that they simply have no notion that education might enable them to set it down.

Basic and community education

Colombia offers an illustration of the intractable problems to be faced, the methods typically adopted to tackle them, and also of an unusually successful programme of radio education for adults which has stimulated emulation in neighbouring countries. Though in the large cities adults attend *bachillerato* classes and follow university and vocational courses in their spare time, in Colombia the provision of general education to meet the specific needs of adults in the modern world practically does not exist. The Workers' University in Cali provides evening courses in co-operative and trade-union studies, and maintains a residential centre in the country for short courses. Some universities, for example the University of the Andes, accept occasional external adult students into the courses and as the demand arises organize special courses to meet the needs of particular groups, such as senior business officials or the staff of an enterprise. Anything in the nature of an adult education campaign at the moment is largely confined to the rural areas. The population is almost equally divided between the town and the country as a result of the movement of population which began some thirty years ago and still continues. The majority of rural inhabitants live in isolated homesteads on the patch of ground which provides their livelihood. Only a small proportion live in concentrations, village or town. Rough road and track, almost impassable during the rains, make communications difficult. Life is hard and impoverished, little more than primitive, dependent on rudimentary and irrational methods of cultivation. Much of the land is severely eroded and some barely usable. Illiteracy is widespread, and there is little desire to learn to read and write. To escape the wretched monotony of existing, the lack of any cultural outlet, some *campesinos* resort to the rural bars, where they stupefy themselves with quantities of *chicha* and *guarapo*. There is no expectation of change, and no concept that improvement may be possible. Some form of education in the basic techniques of modern life and some preparation for community change are essential prerequisites of social and economic development plans, and necessary safeguards against social disorder and violence.

There is no single organization responsible for basic education and community development, nor any co-ordinating body linking the various institutions involved, though the Department of Planning and Technical Services of the Education Ministry has attempted to obtain the co-operation of the various ministries concerned. The Literacy and Fundamental Education Section of the Ministry of Education on its creation in 1958 took over the literacy programme which had begun in 1948. This Section maintains over thirteen hundred centres for night classes for adults, as well as twenty-one full-time literacy centres in Antioquia and Boyaca, and adult classes in parish schools and voluntary centres. It also administers some twenty fundamental education teams, each consisting of an education expert, an agricultural specialist, a home-improvement adviser and a health education assistant, one in each department and three in the Special District of Bogotá. It has a small team of specialists in techniques of teaching illiterates who, for example in 1962, trained some thirteen thousand persons as instructors. These included students and teachers, members of the armed forces, priests and housewives, who afterwards helped in voluntary classes. The Section also gives support to secondary and normal schools whose students are obliged by ministerial decree to give seventy-two hours during the last two years of their studies to literacy classes and community development work. The Section has published a series of booklets designed to help the literacy teacher, such as the *Manual del Alfabetizada* and *Fundamentos sobre Alfabetización Funcional*, and is in process of publishing four readers for recent literates based on the experimental reading books of the Latin American Centre for Fundamental Education and Community Development, CREFAL.

The budget of the Section is less than 4 million pesos a year, which is quite inadequate to meet even urgent needs, which include the establishment of some five thousand new centres as well as the production of some quarter of a million notebooks and reading manuals and follow-up material, not to mention the starting of rural libraries. It is improbable that substantial additional funds will be made available in the budget of the Ministry of Education, particularly as the official view is that the cause of illiteracy lies in the inadequacy of the primary schools, and the solution in providing adequate primary education (Gomez Valderrama, 1964).

In effect the *núcleos escolares* already described are making an important contribution to the solution of the problem of fundamental education, some thirteen thousand adults and young people having passed through them in 1962. Other types of schools controlled by the Ministry of Education contribute to community development, for example the schools for rural housewives which offer courses in home improvement, and particularly those for training instructors in various skills, the *Escuelas Normales Rurales* and the *Institutos Superiores de Orientación Rural* at Usaquen and Pamplona. Although not controlled by the Ministry of Education, the efforts of the students and staffs of some universities, including the National University and the Universities of the Andes, del Valle, and of Antioquia, in aid of community development are of particular significance, because they bring the future leaders of the country in touch with rural problems.

Basic and community education

The *División de Acción Comunal*, which began in the Ministry of Education in 1959, was tranferred to the Ministry of Home Affairs in 1960. The function of this division is to plan and help to carry out community projects which call for the co-ordinated effort of the community, the State and private organizations, and at the same time to provide the technical advice and training to ensure the success of the projects. It has performed this role by instigating social and economic studies, which are the essential prerequisite of any community project, by organizing training courses both for local leaders and government officials, by producing printed information and teaching materials, and by supplying technical expertise and advice. It has also been responsible for making agreements and contracts with public and private organizations participating in community development, and particularly with the American relief organization CARE, and also with the government of the Netherlands. It was originally through the good offices of CARE that considerable numbers of Peace Corps volunteers came to Colombia to work each for two years in various community projects, and especially in the improvement of cultivation, the construction of cheap housing, and the planning and building of rural roads and bridges. The Netherlands Government provided a balanced team of experts to work towards the all-round improvement of a single community, which might serve as a model for development. The Division has a budget of less than that of the Literacy Section of the Ministry of Education, and lack of funds certainly accounts for its failure to make a very great impact on the problem. The foreign teams, however, who are not financially hamstrung, also have not had complete success. In terms of material achievements they have not failed, but they have not invariably carried the community with them, and at times have provoked antagonism. They have not always sparked off the desire for change, or set in motion the educational process which can lead to improving permanently the conditions and standards of living.

The Ministry of Agriculture, as might be expected, has been involved in rural adult education since 1946, when the Division of Agricultural Extension was inaugurated. In 1960 this was reorganized with four sections: that of programmes for adults, 4-S or Young Farmers Clubs, Home Improvement, and Publications and Information, working at national, departmental and local levels. These sections are staffed by specialists, some of whom have been trained abroad. The extension officers perform their work with adults through farm visits and personal advice, meetings, demonstrations and field days, and by encouraging co-operative activity. In 1963 five agricultural co-operatives were already functioning and thirteen more were projected.

There are over six hundred young farmers' clubs under the name of 4-S – *Saber, Sentimiento, Servicio, Salud* (Knowledge, Feeling, Service, and Health) – with more than twelve thousand members of both sexes. The boys and girls carry out various projects including poultry-rearing, bee-keeping, the breeding of cattle and pigs, the cultivation of cocoa, maize and potatoes, and the improvement of homesteads, under the guidance of their clubs. The United States has given considerable aid to these young peoples' clubs through donations of chickens and farm animals, beehives, equipment for carpentry, cement-block making and sewing machines, as well as by providing Peace Corps volunteers. The Home Improvement section has encouraged the formation of some seventy clubs for housewives, while the section for Publications and Information, in addition to publishing various educational pamphlets, has organized regular radio and television programmes designed to improve the farmers' knowledge of modern techniques and scientific methods, and to broaden his educational background.

On an even greater scale than the work of the Ministry of Agriculture is that of the Federation of Coffee Growers which began in 1958. This organization has succeeded in obtaining the active co-operation of over half the municipalities in the coffee-growing departments, and has about seventy branches serving over seventy thousand farms. Its educational work is directed towards improving the techniques of coffee growing, but also towards diversifying the crops grown on farms, which have in the past depended almost exclusively on the coffee bean, and to encourage minor industries. Similar work on a smaller scale, together with the training of instructors, is performed by the Cotton Development and the Tobacco Development Institutes, while the development plans of the *Banco Cafetero*, the *Caja Agraria*, the Agricultural Credit Bank and the Institute for Agrarian Reform involve some educational work and co-operation with existing extension services.

The radio schools movement

The most impressive effort in rural education is the work of *Acción Cultural Popular* working through Radio Sutatenza. This organization in 1962 had 22,145 *escuelas radiofónicas*, radio listening schools, with an average of almost one hundred students each. From 1954 up to 1961 it claims to have taught 184,206 people to read and write, and to have trained over a third of a million in some branch of rural economy. The beginnings of the movement were very modest. In 1947 Padre José Joaquin Salcedo arrived at Sutatenza, a typical backward, scattered rural parish of some seven thousand inhabitants, about three hours' car drive from Bogotá. Stirred by the almost inhuman conditions in which the people lived, this priest resolved to bring about changes, not by preaching against drunkenness, ignorance and poverty, but by persuading the community to improve itself. He first used film, showing through the screen a new world which attracted the attention of the people. The vital step of stirring their interest was achieved in this way. A month later he made experiments in establishing a radio link between outlying homesteads and a central point in the village of Sutatenza, which led to the installation of three receiving sets, and in consequence to the first *escuelas radiofónicas*. He appealed for voluntary help to build a studio and he recorded and broadcast the voices of all who came to give service. By such devices local interest was built up. In three years 200,000 pesos had been collected and a movement was started.

In the meantime Father Salcedo had sought the help and collaboration of the United Nations, the United States and the Philips Company of Holland, to such effect that by 1951 three transmitters and over five thousand receivers were installed, a building was completed and *Acción Cultural Popular* was legally constituted. From then onwards progress has been continuous. In 1954 a second station began to function in Belencito, and in 1955 Radio Sutatenza began to broadcast from Bogotá. In 1958 the weekly bulletin *El Campesino* appeared for the first time with a distribution of twenty-nine thousand copies, which by 1963 had reached an accumulated total of nearly seventeen millions. Enormous numbers of reading manuals and textbooks were also produced. Training schools for local auxiliaries, instructors and organizers were established at Sutatenza and in Medellin. From a local effort, which attracted international aid and an annual grant of 5 million pesos from the national treasury, a great organization had been built up.

There are three elements in the working of the organization. On the ground are the radio schools, centred on a fixed-wavelength radio, located in a convenient home or a village schoolroom not more than twenty or thirty minutes walk from any student. Experience in other places in the world makes the persistence and success of Sutatenza listening groups surprising. The explanation lies, at any rate in part, in the scattered distribution of the rural population. The radio set was the easiest, at times the sole, contact with the outside world. Evidence for this view is supplied by the unexpected fact that such was the demand that provision also had to be made for children of school age who constituted probably more than half the enrolment of the radio schools. Dissatisfaction with local schools and their deficiencies, the physical isolation of the village school, and the aloofness of the village schoolmaster, often a stranger unfamiliar with the community and its ways, were all factors in favour of radio education.

Next at central points come the broadcasting stations, emitting the lessons, not exclusively but at fixed times between programmes of entertainment and news. The fleeting human voice of the broadcast does not, however, carry the whole burden of making contact with the scattered classes. The radio beam is reinforced by the printed word. Readers and textbooks are distributed to the schools, and also the weekly *El Campesino* provides a channel for gossip, news about events, plans and developments, and serves as a more intimate link between those involved in different parts of the movement. The third element is the human element, and especially those working in the field, in touch with the schools. Probably the most important is the parish priest. If Father Salcedo had not been followed by successors who also dedicated themselves to the movement the outcome would have been different. Not that the priest was without helpers, management boards, paid, trained organizers, technicians available centrally to keep the sets in working order, and voluntary auxiliaries working as class secretaries. All these have become important, even essential, but the parish priest has been the stable figure. Where schools operate under the priest's eye they persist and produce effective results. It is the degree of his interest which determines the level of achievement.

Acción Cultural Popular is not simply a literacy movement, though, as has been pointed out, it has achieved significant results in that field. It claims credit for progress in a number of other activities. An independent investigation into the effects of the radio schools in three sample places suggests that there is some relation between the improvements achieved in these communities and the work of the Sutatenza schools (Torres Restrepo and Corredor Rodriguez, 1961). For example, the village of Mantua, which has the most effective school organization and the most dynamic local leadership of the three places chosen, shows a much higher degree of home improvement in such things as the walls, kitchen and furniture than the other two places. Sutatenza, however, with a less enthusiastic community, but well provided with technical experts, comes ahead in the provision of services such as water, latrines and wash-houses. A similar pattern can be seen in the use of food and drinks. In all except the consumption of fruit, Guatique, a parish without a community organization and with only a few irregular radio schools, falls behind Sutatenza and Mantua, where nearly everyone consumes eggs, meat and chicken on at least five days in a week.

Of course it may be questionable which comes first, the school or the higher standard of nourishment, but in health and agricultural techniques the correlation of cause and effect can be traced with more certainty. The practice of protective health measures, such, for example, as vaccination against typhus, diphtheria, whooping cough and so on, is much more widespread in Sutatenza and Mantua, and the influence of education is emphasized here by the fact that Sutatenza, which has been the centre of the health campaign carried out jointly by *Acción Cultural Popular* and the Health Service, has the highest percentage of people vaccinated. Again the same picture in counter-erosion measures and soil improvement. Contour ploughing and sowing and the application of some form of fertilizer are now almost universal in Mantua and Sutatenza, where previously erosion and soil exhaustion were among the main causes of poverty. Similar differences can be seen in the extent to which hens, dairy cattle and pigs are reared, and in the methods and results achieved. These are material achievements which can be attributed in some degree to the influence of *Acción Cultural Popular*. At the same time there have been changes in attitudes. Formerly, when illiteracy was common, it carried no stigma. Now the inability to read and write is considered a reason for shame. In the past, homes were huts of mud and straw, with no conveniences and no adornments. Today the homestead is a matter of prestige. It is reported that in Mantua a group of houses isolated high in the cordillera and deprived of an *escuela radiofónica*, observing the improved walls and roofs of the houses in the valley below, and the installation of concrete surrounds and gardens, felt bound to follow suit in order to maintain their status and the prestige of the parish. There has also been a change towards willingness to adopt new agricultural techniques. From generation to generation agriculture has been carried on in the same inadequate way. Now farmers are aware of the dangers of failing to preserve the soil and to keep it in good heart. They know about the damage caused by various pests and diseases. They are willing to use new methods and use fertilizers and chemical sprays. They are taking more pride in good husbandry and through it seeking a higher standard of living.

The Colombian movement stimulated parallel schemes elsewhere, and in due course the creation of a Latin American Federation of Radio Schools. At a Congress held in 1963 three distinct attitudes became apparent. As might be expected Colombia took a conservative stand, attributing the success of the Sutatenza project to the parish priest as the principal agent. Peru, Bolivia and Ecuador were interested in their own racial divisions and in the radio as a possible means of integrating the non-Spanish speaking Indians into the process of development, and shortly after the congress Radio Lima did in fact start an adult education programme for the benefit of Indians, providing some ten thousand sets to homesteads and another thirteen hundred to schools to enable listening groups to receive the broadcasts. Venezuela, Chile and Mexico proposed a frankly liberal political view, stressing the role to be played by the laity, the importance of programmes directed to the growing mass of urban dwellers, and the overriding objective of *hacer patria*, forming the motherland. Mexico has launched another patriotic campaign to eradicate illiteracy, this time through the medium of television, requiring eleven commercial stations to allot programme time to this purpose. Radio has also played a part in the Venezuelan campaign which recorded a million and a third new literates in four years, and claimed that the remaining 13 per cent of the population still illiterate would not be so after another four years.

Rural development and education

Nevertheless, in spite of the achievements which *Acción Cultural Popular* and radio fundamental education schools can claim in Colombia and her sister republics, community development is still far from solving the social problems of the countryside and far from abolishing poverty. The old ways still have a powerful hold. The simplicity of the life of country people living together in isolated homesteads makes it difficult for them to change their ways in any basic manner, and a slow process. New ideas are certainly astir, but they have not yet brought radical changes in standards of living, and this perhaps cannot be done simply by teaching a few new techniques and instilling the habits of self help. Projects for community development are no more than parochial concepts. It is true that the conditions of the countryside, particularly during the last two decades, militate against any sort of progress, and also that work at the grass roots must come first. In these circumstances the guerrilla leader, who, benefiting from the influence of the *núcleo escolar*, becomes a chairman of committee, represents an achievement. A parish such as Sutatenza, which recovers its self-respect through adult education, is worthy of commendation. But these hardly amount to major historical events. The educational thinking is not on a sufficiently broad scale to make any fundamental impact on rural development. The vision of a completely new and better way of life for the country is missing. In part this may be because some of the ideas for rural reform are equally devoid of any worthwhile purpose, beyond providing an attractive political platform. The breaking up of large estates, the handing over of small parcels of land to peasant proprietors, and even the colonization of new land in small plots is not going to set the rural economy booming and turn every holding into an emerald mine. Some of the best-intentioned reforms result in holdings too small to be viable. The best that can be aimed at in this kind of framework is to give the farmer the basic tools of knowledge and technique to enable him to feed himself and his family a little better. Though this is no mean aim, such micro-metrical schemes reflect economic policies which, it is said, sacrifice foreign exchange derived from the traditional sources of wealth of the country, coffee and other agricultural products, for the sake of building up the industrial sector. The countryside is being exploited by the town. Dr Dolcey Garcés, an economist who received his postgraduate training at the London School of Economics, wrote a letter to the national newspaper *El Siglo* in January 1966, in which he accused Ministers of thinking too much about exporting manufactured goods when they should 'think more of the primary products such as beef, fish, wool, etc., because they should remember that the material progress of Colombia in this century has been due, whether for good or evil, to one primary product, coffee'.

Such strictures may not be entirely justified. Plans do exist for major developments of the countryside; there are those of the *Caja Agraria*, and those of the Institute for Agricultural Reform, INCORA, backed by extensive North American aid. In these cases the criticism might take a different line. Though INCORA is much concerned with setting up small farmers, some of the schemes of the two organizations call for advanced engineering or managerial skills quite beyond the capacities of local people. They are produced by experts concerned only with their own field of ideas and unaware of the attitudes, shortcomings and prejudices of the people of the area affected. The experts may well be right. Theirs are projects which will make a real difference in the standards and ways of life of the countryside. It is the educationists who are falling behind. They are not helping the human beings who have to live with the schemes to come to terms with them. Community education is not co-ordinated with major development plans. The rural and agricultural educational system in Colombia, as in other South American countries, is inadequate for the task of preparing a genera-tion skilled in modern techniques, capable of coping with techno-logical innovations, and endowed with the understanding necessary to transform rural life and enable it to resist the blandishments of the town. This was substantially the view expressed by the institute for Economic and Social Development Studies of Paris in the evalua-tion of educational progress it undertook in 1963 for the OAS. The Institute pointed out the shortcomings of literacy campaigns in

Latin America, and stressed the need for integrating community development programmes with specific economic projects.

The rural primary schools, other than the *núcleos escolares*, are very weak. Reichel-Dolmatoff has described the village schools in the Guajira peninsula in the north-east of Colombia, staffed by teachers who belong to leading local families, limited in outlook and concerned with preserving local values. There teachers were very critical of official programmes and antagonistic to such government initiatives as reafforestation or the establishment of kitchen gardens in schools. They conveyed to the children their attitude that manual work was degrading and that anyone who attended school merited white-collar employment (Reichel-Dolmatoff, 1961). Wastage in rural schools is tremendous and the average child spends only a couple of years in school. Thomas Balogh noted how impermanent was the effect of the rural primary course on children who spent only a fleeting moment in class. He suggested that fundamental changes were needed, and that the complete waste of the limited supply of teachers which occurs in the present situation might be avoided by raising the school-entry age to ten, or even twelve, when the child would be more mature and capable of benefiting from the instruction (Balogh, 1965). The *escuelas de práctica agropecuaria*, into which considerable resources have been poured to train future farmers, are generally a deception. They take only a minute proportion of the rural young people, and those who are accepted not infrequently make use of the training to escape from the farm. Similarly, extension work is limited and 'in-service' training poorly developed. At the intermediate stage, agricultural secondary schools hardly exist. Higher education is in one sense better developed than the other sectors. Throughout Latin America there are fifty-one Faculties of Agriculture, twenty-five of Veterinary Science and nine of Forestry, and Colombia has a fair share of these, as well as a very fine agricultural library in the National Faculty of Agriculture at Medellin. However, the production of graduates amounts to only about one in every eleven thousand of population. In 1961 the Colombian National University, in association with the National Committee for Higher Agricultural Education, made a study of the situation in Colombia in which was noted the lack of interest on the part of ambitious young people in agriculture as a profession, resulting in the schools being unable to fill many more than two-thirds of the available places. The study also lamented the lack of effective co-ordination of internal teaching, research and extension work (*La Educación*, Nos. 25–26, 1962). The rural educational system as it exists does not promise to transform the rich agricultural potentiality of Colombia into a modern, efficient reality.

For the moment nothing can be claimed except that a start of a process has been made. An idea of the possibility of development has been sown, and at the same time a certain unrest, a dissatisfaction with things as they are have appeared. There are models and pilot projects, but to launch campaigns without resources of ideas the material to carry them through may prove dangerous. If the gap between expectations and needs on the one hand, and performance on the other does not become narrower, a rejection of *Acción Cultural Popular* is not hard to imagine. Since communities which have lifted themselves even a little out of their former wretched torpor will not fall without protest again into the rut, this discontent may turn against recognized government and society, and seek in fresh violence what it failed to achieve by peaceful means, and the slow action of education.

8

Overseas aid and
education

In Peru the most sought-after secondary school is Markham College, named after a British Ambassador and scholar. This is one of some twenty or so British-type schools which exist in Latin America, and there are numerous others with special links with the United States of America, France, Italy, Germany, Spain, Israel and so on. Although some of these schools originated in the need to make provision for their own children of the expatriate communities engaged in mining, railway construction, oil exploitation or fruit farming, they all accept local children. Many, indeed, were created and are maintained by groups of local citizens who, still thinking of Europe as a cultural home, held its education particularly in high esteem, and valued the qualifications and professional integrity of foreign teachers above their own. In some cases the English, French and German languages are an attraction as useful tools in the modern world and as the essential basis for further study in North American or European universities. Without overtly making the schools instruments of cultural foreign policy, interested embassies usually are most sympathetic towards the efforts of 'their' schools. Secondary education generally remains the privilege of influential minorities and neither ministries nor parents are unaware that the overseas sponsors of the foreign schools hope to exercise some kind of influence in Latin America through them, an influence which in certain circumstances could have political advantage. Indeed, not a few of the present leaders have enjoyed the facilities of foreign schools and have a particular understanding of the countries associated with them (Fitzgerald, 1957). The flags are therefore still displayed when the son of a president is enrolled, and great is the gloom, though not necessarily on the part of the class teacher, should he later be withdrawn because he is not making progress.

Whether the foreign schools are supported materially by overseas governments or not, they constitute a form of technical aid to the host country. Generally they achieve a deservedly good reputation, partly because they introduce into Latin America methods which combine concern with character training and tested educational ideas, but mainly because they employ qualified foreign teachers. Normally the proportion of foreign staff employed is limited by law, but can run to 50 per cent, as in the cases, for example, of the French *lycée*, which operates under the terms of a cultural convention, or the German-sponsored Andino College in Bogotá. Normally the foreign-type schools follow the curriculum laid down by the Ministry of Education of the host country. In Colombia this is required by ministry regulations. Under the terms of bi-lateral agreements some also offer an overseas programme, ostensibly for expatriate pupils, though without excluding local children. A few schools, not permitting the limits of the possible to bar them from supplementing income, even attempt two overseas courses, catering for, say, British and United States children as well as Colombian. Normally the overseas teachers give their lessons in their own language, in spite of the fact that this may infringe educational regulations, which normally require all subjects except foreign languages to be taught in the national language.

Although these schools are making possibly an essential contribution to the secondary sector, they are not immune from criticism. Courtesy seems to conceal open complaint, yet it may be suspected that education ministers are somewhat embarrassed at having to rely on foreign schools to such an extent. In normal times the schools do not spark off the sort of resentment felt against select schools founded by the former administering power in recently independent countries elsewhere in the world. Nevertheless, no country can relish the best schools being run more or less by foreigners. People think that foreigners cannot be entirely sympathetic towards national aspirations, but introduce elements of rivalry and disruption, which impede the emergence of common purposes, even though the fissiparous influences are usually exercised unintentionally and unwittingly, and may be counterbalanced by the professional competence of the expatriates. It is less easy to relax the tensions which arise from disparities often existing between the salaries of expatriate and national teachers. The resentment may be at least as great on the part of parents as of local teachers, if they are unwilling to understand why they should pay as much as three times the local rates for overseas personnel.

British and American professional teachers do not differ from other nationalities in expecting to receive no less than their home, scale of pay, and in addition an overseas allowance to cover additional expenses caused by working abroad for limited periods. They also, of course, expect paid passages to the post, and certain social benefits such as free medical treatment, which they might expect at home. With the present world demand for qualified teachers they go elsewhere if Latin America cannot offer them attractive terms. In some cases, for example in some French and German schools, part of the salary is paid in the teachers' home country. This may make it possible to hide the extent of the disparities, particularly if the amounts are derived from overseas government aid and do not appear in the schools' budgets. These procedures, however, do not remove the problem of different status levels. Guyana had a similar problem inherited from the colonial era, when the salary scales of official secondary schools were originally based on overseas recruitment. These scales, which persist in some measure, constitute a bone of contention between those who enjoy them and teachers in less fortunate schools on lower scales. In Latin America the salaries in most cases have to be paid by the parents, and consequently the foreign schools are among the most expensive, open only to those of high economic status in the community.

Supplying secondary school teachers is probably the most effective form of aid the advanced can offer the developing countries, providing the aid fits in with the plans for the development of the educational systems. So long as Latin American republics depend so much on private secondary schools presumably the foreign schools will contribute something to social and economic progress. However, the segregation of foreign teachers in select schools divorced from the rest of the system, and the almost complete absence of foreign qualified personnel from the official schools cannot be as effective a means of helping the development of improved standards as their dispersal through the secondary school system. The schools may be models, but models which cannot be copied because of lack of resources. Indeed, because they are absorbing a substantial part of the resources the community is putting into secondary education, they are in fact hindering wider development, and perpetuating the values and profound social divisions of the past. Aid to foreign-type schools may currently be a justifiable tool of political expediency, but it is not necessarily the best way anywhere of helping the Latin American secondary school systems to develop, and the risks involved in those countries which eventually choose a more revolutionary pace of social change are too obvious to need further comment.

International experts

The foreign schools, however, are a relatively small part of the overseas participation in South American educational development. A good deal of the programme of expansion and reform of school education has depended on the support of Unesco, the Organization of American States and the international foundations, while almost every private university and some of the official institutions of higher education are quite familiar with the representatives of the great North American philanthropic organizations. Most governments receive the aid as indispensable and accept that little could be done without it. Yet even South Americans with broad international sympathies who were quite ready to concede that the advanced nations are capable of solving everyone's problems, are beginning to have doubts. More than one critic has called in question the effectiveness of some international aid. The results have not been outstanding. Advice is in abundance, but too often the means to implement it are completely lacking. The so-called experts if highly qualified in their own limited specialist field, are usually not knowledgeable about the environment in which they work, and may lack the flexibility of mind necessary to see problems through different eyes which comes from contact with other peoples. They cost too much, and some earn more than the ministers they serve. The title of international expert has often been too easily conferred, and the contribution made to development by experts from abroad has not only been sometimes ineffectual but harmful, in so far as they have diverted attention from a proper appraisal of the problems. And the bigger the aid, the more harmful it has sometimes been. It is not adequately recognized that the visiting expert must make himself equally knowledgeable about the country in which he is working, and he must have that sympathetic understanding and insight into those with whom he is working to make his lead acceptable. The job calls for a professional approach and not merely an attitude of vague goodwill.

In spite of the devoted contribution of many foreign volunteers and officials, some of the critical doubts have taken a xenophobic turn. Much of the aid comes from North America, and it is, perhaps, inevitable that thinking and planning has been influenced unduly by United States ideas and practices, even if not by almost obsessive anti-communist preoccupations. Some fear that Colombia, for example, the nearest republic to the great neighbour and the projected showpiece of the Alliance for Progress, is being browbeaten, so to speak, into accepting solutions not truly compatible with national aspirations. They say the help accepted is not only alien but of poor quality, and they point to the example of the team working in educational television, which includes sheer amateurs lacking specialized experience both of television and of primary schools, whose boldness in presuming to teach others in a foreign country could only be put down to naïvety.

There are those among the most educated Colombians who intellectually reject North American aid entirely, claiming that it is utterly foreign and cannot provide the basis for growth without destroying national identity and self-respect. They would prefer a slower pace without aid. Nor can this point of view be attributed solely to the minority who have a vested interest in preserving the *status quo*; on the contrary, it is widely held that Americans lend their influence in support of the privileged. It is rather a claim for a form of aid responsive to Colombian needs, which does not impose alien solutions identified through alien eyes. This sort of understanding, it must be admitted, is not easy to achieve, and up to the present encouragement has not always been forthcoming from the Colombians. It has often not been possible to identify real needs in any particular field, or to obtain any indication of an order of priorities of educational needs, and attempts to discover the main sectors in which help would be welcome and useful are likely to meet with the bland response that help is needed in every field. When initiative in starting aid projects really comes from the Latin American side in the form of specific planned requests prepared by professional experts, there is the opportunity for more genuine partnership, though it would be too much to hope that this will restrain the flow of indiscriminate offers from overseas which at present cause confusion and some misunderstanding. It makes even more imperative the necessity for overseas experts to obtain a deep understanding of the country in which they work.

Study abroad

All undeveloped and partially developed countries depend in some measure on a programme of study abroad to meet their needs of trained manpower, and overseas institutions of higher education are making an increasing contribution to their development. In the past the brighter scholars from colonies were normally sent to the metropolitan countries for higher studies, and a tradition of study abroad was established, which having gained esteem because many of the new leaders have benefited from it, easily survived the change of régime and the appearance of national universities. The abrupt withdrawal of administrators and technical specialists in many instances intensified the need for emergency courses, which the new states could not provide. The recent University of Guyana has not the facilities to absorb all who seek places and the unsuccessful ones are obliged to go abroad for what they cannot find at home. It is estimated that Guyana will require an average of three hundred university graduates a year during the period up to 1971. The annual intake of the university over this period will be about one hundred and fifty. In 1967 there were one hundred and forty-one Guayanese undergraduates studying for degrees in Britain alone (British Council, 1967). Even if all those abroad after completing courses returned to Guyana to join the local graduates, the needs for specialists could not be met and it is evident that it will be necessary to extend the programme for overseas study for some time to come.

In Latin America too there has been a tradition of study abroad, though the origins were somewhat different. The link with Europe was not completely severed, at least for a small section of the population who thought of themselves culturally as heirs of Greece and Rome, eighteenth-century France, or even of twentieth-century Germany. Some families with the means to do so would send their sons if not their daughters to the universities of France, Spain and Germany. For others the great country to the north exercised a strong attraction. In the cities it is· not rare to find doctors, engineers and businessmen, who have had some training in the United States. During the first decade of its existence the Colombian University of the Andes sent its students for their two final years before graduation to various North American universities. The Andes is one of the universities which have worked particularly closely with the *Instituto Colombiano de Especialización Técnica en el Exterior*, or ICETEX, as it is generally called. This organization, which is responsible for all Colombia's programme of study overseas, has already attracted a good deal of attention from neighbouring countries and justifies more detailed description.

In 1943 Dr Gabriel Betancur Mejia, then a student at the University of Syracuse, presented a thesis in which were contained the germs of the idea of ICETEX. The chances of obtaining a university degree in Colombia were limited. The privilege was open only to those in the higher income groups, and the careers to which university courses led went little beyond the traditional fields of medicine, law and civil engineering. The few scholarships offered by the Government and the municipalities were usually acquired by those who had some pull or could benefit from political influence. The opportunities for postgraduate specialization were even more scarce. The challenge of a technological age just beginning and of rising social expectations were not met. The situation was ripe for a new organization which would answer the call of less privileged social groups for higher education, and at the same time supply the country's increasing demands for highly trained personnel. The idea sown in 1943 became a fact in 1952 when the Government nominated a Director and supplied funds to enable the Colombian Institute for Advanced Study Abroad to begin work. In 1953 the first thirty-two Colombians were sent abroad with scholarships to train in specialities urgently required by the economy and education system of the country. Ten years later the annual number of students helped in some way to study abroad was around three thousand, and those receiving loans to study in Colombian universities topped one thousand. By this time ICETEX had developed a wide range of schemes to facilitate higher study both overseas and at home.

Early in its history ICETEX established a loan system as its principal means of operation. Loans are available to graduates, normal teachers and agricultural instructors who can offer proof that they are suitable both academically and in character and experience to benefit by advanced courses, and whose proposed studies will be of evident use to the country. A special programme to encourage higher studies by university teachers was negotiated with the Association of Universities in 1960. Under this scheme 70 per cent of the cost of the course of study is lent to the university interested, which must find the remaining costs. Those teachers who benefit undertake to return to a teaching post at the university for a period double the length of the studies undertaken, failing which they may be called upon to repay the loan themselves. The usual form of loan, however, may be total, sufficient to cover the whole expenses of the courses including passages and living expenses, or partial, to be supplemented from the students' own resources, or by scholarship from other sources. The minimum period for loans is six months and the maximum two years. Repayment of the loans by instalments starts three months after the date the loan ends. An interest at 3 per cent is charged on the remaining unpaid portion, except for those who are engaged in not less than three hours' teaching or educational administration a week, and who are not behind in their repayments. Interest at 8 per cent is charged on instalments not paid when due. As all loans are insured, the debts of those who die are cancelled.

Through the medium of the *Comité Nacional de Becas*, the National Scholarships Committee, which was set up by the Government in 1958, ICETEX administers scholarships offered to Colombia by various international bodies such as the Organization of American States, Unesco and various universities of the United States, and co-operates in the scholarship programmes of Germany, Brazil, Belgium, Spain, Japan, France, Holland, Israel, Italy, the United Kingdom, Switzerland and the Scandinavian countries. Similarly, scholarships for artists to study abroad offered by the Ministry of Education are dealt with by ICETEX. It is considered a matter of national pride that promising artists should be enabled to improve their talents by contact with artists overseas, and grants rather than loans are thought appropriate as the artist is not assured of a market for his works in Colombia which could guarantee his ability to repay. Help is also given to students going abroad for higher studies at their own expense, through facilities for obtaining foreign currency at the official rate instead of at the free rate which has been much less favourable. The Institute operates a loan scheme for those who wish to pursue higher studies in Colombia. The criterion of selection is intellectual capacity and personal merit only. This type of loan is renewable each year provided the student obtains an average of 70 per cent of the marks in the yearly examinations, and is repayable in instalments over three or five years, beginning twelve months after the course of study ends.

Impressed by the experience of ICETEX, in 1963 the Bank of the Republic authorized a special low rate of interest of 2 per cent on loans made by commercial banks for the purpose of facilitating study within Colombia. This programme is well under way, using methods similar to ICETEX, which acts as adviser and assessor in each case. The loans range from 400 pesos monthly for university students to 1,500 pesos for married graduate students, together with amounts to cover registration, fees and books. They are renewable each year on the same terms as ICETEX home loans, and repayment has to be made over a period equal to twice the length of the period of study, with a maximum of ten years, starting twelve months after the course ends. The banks' loan programme is expected to expand rapidly.

As schemes develop a series of auxiliary services became necessary. The Committee for Study Abroad first came into being because of the necessity for screening the requests for dollars at the official rate. It quickly took over the task of supervising the academic progress of the students abroad under the various schemes, loan, scholarship or exchange facilities, all of which require evidence of satisfactory progress. For students in the United States this is not a difficult undertaking because of the credit system and the common use of student counsellors. Nor is it burdensome in countries such as Great Britain where ICETEX has been able to make an agreement with the British Council to obtain regular reports. In Germany, France and Italy, however, the tradition of academic freedom for students raises some thorny problems. An advisory and information service which could offer guidance on overseas educational institutions was an obvious essential from an early date. The Institute's documentation centre can deal at any rate with most preliminary inquiries and the International Relations Office can obtain more detailed information which may become necessary from the cultural mission of the country concerned. More recently, filling a gap revealed by the survey of requirements of highly trained personnel, ICETEX has set up an employment service for graduates and professional people in an effort to ensure in the first place that the skills of those who return from abroad are not wasted through unemployment resulting from the lack of information about the opportunities open. Associated with this service will be a directory of professional specialists.

The money to administer these various schemes for training abroad and at home, apart from repayment of loans, comes from three main sources. About a seventh of the income has recently been earned in the form of honoraria for services, rents, interest on loans and so on. Government grants-in-aid have accounted for two-sevenths, though estimates up to 1968 suggested that this proportion was expected to rise steeply. However, up to 1966 the major part of the income was derived from trust funds. By 1965 seventy-two trust funds were administered by ICETEX on behalf of public and private entities. The sums provided are in nearly all cases used for loans rather than grants. Normally the agreements with ICETEX are for a minimum of five years so that a continuous plan can be developed. Each fund is controlled by a board consisting of representatives of the donor institution under the chairmanship of the Director of ICETEX. The main sources of trust funds are the Association of Universities, together with the University of the Andes and the National University, the Ministries of Education and Mines, the National Telecommunications Board, the National Petroleum Company and the National Federation of Coffee Growers. In 1962 ICETEX undertook the administration of the national funds invested in the *Instituto Linguistico Colombo-Americano*, ILCA, which was established by agreement between the Ministry of Education, the University of California and the United States Government, in order to provide in-service courses in new methods of language teaching, and at the same time to produce a six-year language course based on modern linguistic knowledge for use in secondary schools.

It is, of course, to be expected that ICETEX attracts to itself a number of miscellaneous functions connected with student exchange and international student relations. It has an agreement with the United States Government and the universities of the State of Florida setting up a scheme to facilitate exchanges of high school and university students. The Latin American Scholarship Programme of American Universities is conducted in Colombia by ICETEX, which supplement the grants with loans to cover local expenses, and also the expenses of the first and last terms which the conditions of the awards require to be completed in Colombian universities. The Colombian Committee for the 'Experiment in International Living' and for the 'International Association for the Exchange of Students for Technical Experience' are housed in ICETEX, which is also the Colombian agent for the 'Council on Student Travel'. The National Scholarships Committee is responsible for the open scholarship offered to overseas students of the Spanish language at the Seminario Andres Bello of the *Instituto Caro y Cuervo* in Bogotá, and for a scholarship in town and regional planning at the *Universidad del Valle*, both financed by the Ministry of Education, as well as for a scholarship in postgraduate studies in sociology offered by the National University.

Education and Manpower Requirements

The statutes of incorporation required ICETEX to undertake research into the country's needs for highly trained personnel. This was begun in 1961, and four years later the first results were published under the title of *Resources and Requirements for Highly Trained Personnel*. The final document will include a description of the Colombian educational system, and particularly of the facilities for higher education, and also of the social and economic situation of the country. It will give an analysis of the results of the detailed investigation into the employment structure of public and private undertakings, and attempt to establish a relationship between educational services, human resources, and economic development with a view to forecasting the implications of the whole programme of research for the educational and economic policy of the country. ICETEX published its own four-year plan up to 1968 based on these investigations. An increase of almost 70 per cent in the number of specialists trained abroad and in Colombia is expected, though the increase will be more pronounced in the number studying in Colombia, where it will be over 90 per cent. It is anticipated that while the number of awards from overseas sources will rise steadily to 467

in 1968, the number of students going abroad on their own resources and with loans will rise to 1,787 after three years, but in
1968 will begin to drop. The number of students studying in
Colombia with ICETEX help or support from other agencies will
continue at a level somewhat higher than it was in 1965, but the
number benefiting from the bank loans will almost double itself.
Generally speaking less reliance will be placed on overseas study
and on ICETEX's own resources than in the past. A detailed forecast
of the targets in each subject and group of subjects was compiled.
This revealed that the exact sciences and various types of engineering taken as a whole head the list, with agriculture and its related
subjects closely behind, and it is precisely in these fields that the
number of students abroad is expected to fall in 1968, in the face
of the increased numbers who can be catered for in Colombia
(ICETEX, 1966). The plan provides for a pronounced increase in the
minute numbers trained in the past for technician-level appointments. For example, whereas in 1965 the number trained at home
and abroad for *técnica agrícola* and *técnica forestal* was eleven, this
number was expected to rise to sixty-eight in 1968. The figures for
medical laboratory technicians are twenty-three in 1965 and fifty-
five in 1968, and in this particular field Brazil has shown the way to
setting up a laboratory technician-training centre with British
assistance.

In the course of a decade ICETEX has grown, so to speak, into its
clothes. In the first instance it granted loans to a few candidates, a
small portion of those who left Colombia for higher study. Now,
largely because it controls the availability of foreign exchange for
study, and because the international sources of fellowships lend their
co-operation, it goes a long way towards dealing with all Colombians
seeking courses abroad, as indeed it has a statutory right to do. Unlike many other countries, it made the decision from the start that
Colombian awards should be in the form of loans rather than grants,
and it has made good use of this system to increase steadily the number of students who could benefit. Recently it has sponsored a loan
scheme for students at universities and secondary schools in
Colombia, and so has placed itself in an advantageous position for
overlooking both the programme of home as well as overseas awards.
ICETEX has now both the administrative machinery and the knowledge
to implement a plan of study abroad closely geared to the needs of

the country, at any rate in so far as they are revealed by development plans. Those responsible for the organization would certainly subscribe to the liberal view that freedom to seek knowledge wherever it can be found is fundamental, and it is unlikely that a rigid system of control of study will be introduced. Nevertheless, it is manifest that the programme of overseas study must reflect the needs of the country as a whole. The available resources, and particularly the amount of foreign exchange which can be allotted to this programme make it impossible to allow the pattern of overseas study to be dictated entirely by choice exercised by individuals. Although ICETEX was able to give preferential rates of exchange to those whose plans of study were approved, there was no exchange control so that others too could obtain foreign currency by paying the free market rate. In 1966 a new government introduced exchange control, and with it the possibility for ICETEX to control the whole programme of study abroad. It seems that this trend towards the management of overseas study in the light of what are considered the national interests will continue, and that the conditions, so to speak, of the completely free market of entirely personal aspirations now belong to the past.

ICETEX can claim solid achievements which are probably as much a contribution to peaceful social change as to economic development. It changed the accepted though limited system of free grants to a loans system, on the principle that educaton is an investment no less for the individual than for the community. At the same time ICETEX rejected the old network of nepotism and political connections as the most effective means of obtaining educational opportunity, and substituted for it a process of selection depending on intellectual capacity and personal merit. Its success has been impressive enough to attractive imitations. Panama and the Dominican Republic sought ICETEX help in setting up similar organizations, and the *Instituto Peruano de Fomento Educativo* followed ICETEX experience in changing from scholarships to a loan system. In 1964 ICETEX sponsored the first meeting of these organizations in Bogotá where it was resolved to form an *Asociación Latinoamericana de Institutos de Crédito y Fomento Educativo*, the Latin-American Association of Institutes of Educational Credit and Development.

Although this experiment in managing the programme of overseas study has evident advantages, it cannot be said that external aid in either direction has been universally effective. Too often it has been used to buttress the closed traditional educational systems, and to improve the position of those at the apex of society (Pike and Bray, 1960). Even if it turns out that any contribution to educational growth is inevitably a contribution to social progress, whether it is intended or not, it is difficult to see what can be done to offset the powerful attraction the great technological power to the north exercises on those whom it does so much to train. In a letter to the *New York Times* in November 1966 Mr Gregory Henderson of the United Nations Institute for Training and Research pointed out that the value to the United States of the talented immigrants from developing countries might be greater than the total value of the aid programme to these countries. Over fifteen thousand engineers, scientists and doctors entered the United States in 1963 and 1964, and numbers of these came from the continent to the south. Latin America faces perhaps more urgently than other countries from which these specialists came the problem of changing her societies so that they may become more capable, socially and economically, of holding the talents which overseas aid is helping to produce.

Particularly pertinent in this connection are the manpower survey and the efforts which ICETEX undertook to identify and limit the fields of training which are required, and to provide some means of assuring that the trained specialists are in fact properly used on their return home. In recent years training provided abroad is often not completely appropriate to the unique needs of the countries of the overseas students. It is inevitable that the courses Latin American students attend in other countries are primarily designed to fulfil criteria of these countries themselves, and only secondarily to serve the guest students. Seeking to advance on several fronts at the same time the developing countries may be obliged to look elsewhere for specialist training which they cannot provide within their boundaries, to avoid holding up a project. Study abroad has to be accepted in these circumstances. ICETEX is right in clarifying more precisely the specialist fields in which study abroad is essential if progress is to be maintained. It is, moreover, entirely justified in looking forward to a date when the number of students going abroad can be reduced. However, it is becoming increasingly clear that the investment of aid funds in fostering training facilities in the developing country may make a more effective and more durable contribution to development than the award of fellowships abroad.

In Colombia aid schemes which have been initiated following a specific Colombian request, and which are concerned with advancing a particular type of educational institution have already had considerable effect. In rural development the Sutatenza radio schools project owed some of its success to overseas aid being available at the time the problem and the solution had been identified at the village level. In the industrial sector various countries have contributed to the building up of SENA into a vital training institution for the future, just as they are now repeating the operation in helping the Peruvian SENATI. Within SENA, the British undertook a complete project at the Colombian request in the form of a training institution for foundry work, which is not only filling a gap but also will lead to a revolution in the methods of small engineering industries. Similarly, in Peru certain advanced countries have, as it were, adopted particular aspects of the industrial training project. After Britain had led the way in equipping lathe-shops, milling, sheet metal and steel workshops, as well as in providing specialists to train instructors, Germany did the same for motor-vehicle and engineering maintenance, Switzerland for training in precision instruments, and Holland, Denmark and Belgium in other distinct fields. Schemes such as these appeal to Colombians, and indeed to other Latin Americans too, because they are a tangible contribution to progress, a part of organic growth, while training abroad is sometimes seen as inappropriate and impermanent. The offer of fellowships is more open to suspicion of commercial and political motivation, and can in fact impede the emergence of educational institutions in the developing country which comes to depend on international aid for its training needs. And very often award programmes take vital development personnel away from their work for less than essential reasons.

The story of overseas official aid to Colombia is, no doubt, only beginning, and it is too early to draw definite conclusions. Private foreign investment, as distinct from government aid, played a major role up to the Second World War in developing railways, utilities and export industries in every Latin American republic, and since then has been the largest single source of external capital for petroleum exploitation, mining and industries serving the home market. Since 1960 the United States has greatly reinforced this private investment by increasing aid funds through the Inter-American Development Bank and the Alliance for Progress, particularly to encourage efforts at social and educational reform. Experience has been too short to provide evidence that the ultimate objectives of this official investment are always clearly defined or agreed, and much less than the outcome can be foreseen. Some Colombians question whether external aid can be effective without an internal revolution in attitudes, which they claim is an essential prerequisite for social and economic advance. More conservative critics, without going so far, would say that a national revival cannot come from outside. And there are at least a few who suspect that international aid to education, by opening up wider prospects of thought and opportunity may undermine the possibility of complete success for separate national development plans. Similar observations are no doubt made about foreign aid to other South American countries.

9

The Colombian balance
sheet

Since the second Inter-American Conference of Ministers of Education at Lima in 1956 Colombia has made some noteworthy achievements in education. There has been a tremendous increase in the amount of money invested in the public education system. A National Apprenticeship Service has been established on sound lines and the number of people trained for industrial, commercial and agricultural employment has been growing rapidly each year. The Colombian Institute for Higher Study Abroad has proved an effective means of increasing the number of specialists urgently needed and a model for other countries. The last two decades have also seen the birth of numerous universities, including some higher technological institutions, and of the Colombian Association of Universities, which has shown the way towards a reappraisal of the role and effectiveness of the university in Colombia. It would seem that Colombians need no convincing about the value of investment in education as a prime requisite for development. The Minister of Education could say with some satisfaction in his report to Congress for 1963 that the Government was concerned above all with abolishing unjust differences in educational opportunities which were dangerous for the future of the country, and with extending the benefits of education to the greatest number of Colombians possible. The Government considered education as 'a primary and fundamental public service, and at the same time the most decisive instrument to achieve economic development by changing social circumstances'.

Not all Colombians would agree that the Government had cause for satisfaction. Some critics, particularly among university students and teachers, are dubious about the good intentions of ministers. They see in official statements of policy and in the inadequate steps taken to implement plans, sops thrown to the masses to avert attention from the real objectives, which are rather to foster material progress without surrendering the privileges inherited from the past by the more fortunate classes. The statements and reports of the Ministry of Education, they say, are full of high-sounding clichés, which have little relevance to the real situation in Colombia. The programme for improving education in rural areas has not yet borne much fruit. The village primary school is in most places as inadequate as it always was, and the secondary system hardly exists over wide regions. Others would take the view that plans for technical and economic progress are clearly a proper function of government, but would not look with any favour on the social changes which accompany such development. Colombia was making the same mistakes, they would say, as others, and not only in former colonies: teaching people to read. The enlightened, avoiding extremes, would consider educational development both necessary and socially desirable, but would attribute a good deal of the credit for progress achieved to organizations such as ICETEX, the National Apprenticeship Service and the Association of Universities, which are independent of official control. Certainly the sponsors of these institutions are clear and convinced about their importance as instruments of social as well as economic change. They, at any rate, have wittingly engaged themselves in a peaceful revolution. They had the backing of the official world because they appeared to offer an avenue of escape from the violence, which had rent the country for so long and is not entirely past even now. Whether members of successive governments wished it or not, the disruption of the country since 1948 left little choice. They had to respond to the idealism expressed in the Alliance for Progress because they knew that repression alone was profitless. The military and police effort to contain the lawlessness was enormous, and incurred expenditure which could have been better used; while schoolteachers were in short supply, two policemen could be seen on every corner in the cities. Even so, the solution chosen for the troubles has not been only a military one. Over the period of the struggle the budget for education has been steadily growing, indirectly at the expense of the Ministry for War. The national leaders have only latterly given thought to educational planning and the role of education in overall planning, but now attentions have turned in that direction there has been no reluctance to accept the proposition that education is a public matter, and a vital factor in the country's advance. But if this is beyond doubt, it remains open to discuss priorities and timetables.

No less than other countries Colombia faces a series of fundamental choices in educational policy. Should resources be invested in universal primary education, or should those objectives be given up as hopeless and a proportion of the age group abandoned to ignorance? Or should the major effort be concentrated on building up the secondary level, or the institutions of higher education? Should the education provided be mainly general or vocational? Should the emphasis be on letters or on science and mathematics? What proportion of the available resources should be invested in school buildings? And indeed how should available investment be divided between education and economic development, since it is impossible to escape the dilemma that the one cannot be achieved without the other. Decisions cannot be ignored; they are made willy-nilly, by default. Political factors influenced government decisions as much as a realistic assessment of the educational needs of development. In any case, adequate statistical data was not available for planning ahead. Although it is difficult to measure what has been implemented, it is worth attempting to evaluate Colombia's current attainments in education.

The primary school

A convenient yardstick would be the composite index compiled by Frederick Harbison and Charles A. Myers to distinguish among countries in terms of human resource development. The index is simply the arithmetical total of the percentage of the fifteen to nineteen age group enrolled at secondary school, and the percentage of the age group at the third level of education, multiplied by a weight of five. Colombia fell among the countries described as 'partially developed', along with Guatemala, the Dominican Republic, Bolivia, Brazil, Paraguay, Ecuador and Peru, in South America, and, for example, Iran, Malaya, Jamaica and Turkey elsewhere. Above Colombia, among the semi-advanced, were Mexico, Cuba, Costa Rica, Venezuela, Chile and Uruguay, while only Argentina in Latin America figured among the advanced countries at the top of the table (Harbison and Myers, 1964). In terms of *per capita* income

Colombia ranks considerably higher with $298 (US), more or less the same as Mexico, but still less than Chile, Uruguay, Argentina and Venezuela, which comes highest in South America with $851 (US). However, this classification gives only general indications, and in some measure is misleading. Colombia is a land of extreme contrasts and any average indices of development must err in relation to particular regions. Urbanization in Colombia has gone farther than in some other South American countries in the same group. There are numerous medium-sized towns, and in addition to Bogotá, with nearly two million inhabitants, three cities with well over half a million people. Some of these cities have outgrown their basic services, have much overcrowding and unemployment, and do not even bother to hide ills, such as the neglect of the abandoned orphans of the *violencia*, or the exploitation of women and children, which have long disappeared, at least from view, in advanced Western cities. At the same time many of the citizens follow a manner of living which is not inferior culturally or materially to that of their counterparts in Europe and North America. Passing along the modern avenues, the observer does not get the impression that human resources are inadequate for the technological era, and much less that they are barely sufficient to keep the jungle at bay.

At the head of Colombia's educational priorities is the elimination of illiteracy through the expansion of the primary school system. Although enrolment falls below the optimum, and failure to retain children in school leads to many leaving without a firm basis of literacy, the Government is firmly committed to a policy of universal primary education. This is certainly in part a political attitude, which can be traced back to the aspirations of the time of independence at the beginning of the nineteenth century. It is, however, only in this century and particularly during the last two decades that any serious attempt to reach this objective has been made, at a time when other countries outside Latin American faced with similar problems were beginning to have doubts whether a place for every child of primary school age should be given such higher priority. Guyana, almost a neighbour, would not question the ultimate desirability of eliminating illiteracy by giving every child a basic schooling, or of raising the general educational level of the people. The planners, however, have already decided that the best way to these goals is not necessarily the direct path. The Development Plan has pruned ambitions of universal enrolment in the primary school, and has not anticipated the proportion of the age group at school growing beyond 85 per cent by 1981. This does not relieve the Guyana Government of the pressing task of providing forty thousand new places to eliminate overcrowding and to accommodate the increased school age population, but it does relax some of the impossible pressure of the problem. Since buildings are a particularly heavy drain on resources, the Guyana authorities have made a reappraisal of the standards of building previously considered essential, and as a consequence have given construction a lower place in the order of priorities than it might otherwise have had. The emphasis is now on economy and purpose in school design, the elimination of lavish and unnecessary detail, and the use of local in place of imported fittings, and on saving in labour costs by self-help methods. As a result of this choice of priorities it will be possible to divert a greater proportion of available funds to other aspects of primary education and particularly to the training of teachers and the provision of educational materials. Colombia also has used local resources and effort in the building of schools. However, depending on generous North American aid the building programme may have adopted standards higher than economy and basic needs warranted, and it certainly suffered a setback, which may not have been inevitable, when the peso was devalued and when aid was suspended for a time. The point of providing more and more primary places is lost if the children who sit at the extra desks do not receive an education whose quality and duration will enable them to find occupation in the modern sector of the economy. If the economy is not growing sufficiently rapidly to absorb them they have no advantage from their schooling, but on the contrary. In so far as they have become dissatisfied with village life and move to the town to swell the ranks of the urban poor they are worse off than their unschooled brothers who persist in subsistence farming. Frederick Harbison pointed out at an educational conference in Addis Ababa in 1961 that those countries, such as Ghana, Egypt and Nigeria, that had made the most spectacular progress towards eliminating illiteracy while pressing forward with industrialization often encountered serious shortages of high-level manpower as well as the greatest numbers of unemployed. In the long run it might be preferable to move forward on a broad front rather than to concentrate available forces on one or two salients.

Increasing the flow of highly trained manpower may prove a quicker way of achieving universal literacy than putting all the eggs in the primary basket at the expense of secondary and higher education. This way of thinking would suggest that half is too much of the education budget to devote to the first sector, and 1975 too early a date for the achievement of universal enrolment.

Higher education

Turning now to the other end of the educational system, universities in Colombia have enjoyed, together with primary schools, a particularly large share of the national cake. Since 1966 two further universities on the Caribbean coast have appeared bringing the total number in the country to twenty-seven, excluding seventeen other institutions which align themselves with universities by appropriating the title without any sort of official recognition. Of these only a handful were founded earlier than the present century, and eighteen of them were started only within the last twenty years, after the movement for university reform had been under way for some time. This proliferation of universities was not everywhere looked upon as an unmixed blessing. The national newspaper *El Tiempo* referred to it critically in its editorial of 8 December 1964, which suggested that the university had fallen away from its original purpose and high standards, its search for truth and striving for excellence. One outcome of rapid growth at a time of social change was the wave of student unrest during the early sixties which disturbed the university authorities into taking a look at their own backyards. The first number of *Crónica Universitaria*, the organ of the Association of Universities, was devoted almost entirely to an analysis of the crisis of the university, as it was called. Some of the points raised echoed the themes of the earlier reform movement: the instability of the university authorities subject to political pressure and changes; the weakness of university staff lacking teaching skill and any contact with the student body; the inadequacy of finance. At the same time, however, attention was drawn to the irresponsibility of student behaviour and to the disadvantages of attempting to give students representation equal with that of other authorities in the organs of university government. There was no vindictive blame of students, but on the contrary a genuine recognition that the demonstrations were symptoms of deep-seated ills. Nevertheless, the general trend of view was that the claims had gone far enough and were beginning to interfere with the fulfilment of the university's purpose, a forewarning of firmer action to be taken by the new government in 1966.

The analysis also suggested that the university was not making its proper contribution to national development, and this was attributed, somewhat surprisingly perhaps, to the fact that roads, irrigation, and electrification came before higher education in the claims on the budget. The student troubles were less about university autonomy than about the relationship of university development to that of the community. This concern was also behind the expansion of the university sector which took place during the previous years, and behind the forward thinking of the Association of Universities. The Association had been working on three types of plan for expansion of higher education: short-term, medium and long-term, of which the first covering the years 1965–8 was published in 1964. The immediate justification for these projects was the need to make provision for the tremendous increase in candidates for university entrance resulting from the expansion of the primary and secondary schools, and the reform of the *bachillerato*. Above the immediate objectives, however, the introduction to the published short-term plan stressed the vital importance of the university in future economic plans for the country.

While the short-term plan was concerned largely with increasing the number of university places, it recorded dissatisfaction with the current system of admissions based mainly on an entrance examination. As a provisional means of improving the situation it was suggested that aptitude tests should replace examination. At the same time an educational and vocational counselling service was proposed to help students to find the field of special interest for which they were best equipped. The National University adopted intelligence and aptitude tests for entry in 1966, with not entirely satisfactory results, probably due to the limitations of the tests used, inexperience in interpreting scores and the dearth of supporting evidence. The universities of the Andes and of Antioquia set up student guidance units, and the former reorganized its methods of entry and the programmes of the first year of study to help students to discover their bent. In the meantime the Association established an experimental unit staffed by educational psychologists to investigate further the problems of university entrance, and to devise appropriate tests. The unit's view is that tests will prove to be the most suitable method, but that tests of potential character will be of particular importance, and much more useful than achievement tests, in view of the very wide range of efficiency of the secondary schools, and the discrepancies between the cultural backgrounds of the candidates. It was expected that in the long run the unit would become a permanent technical body with the function of devising and administering tests.

In addition to the improvement in university teaching and in libraries, which has already been discussed, the list of priorities in the plan included the need for some division of labour between the universities. The plan indicated certain special groups of subjects in which universities would be called upon to produce more graduates. The specialities were education, agriculture, engineering – particularly mechanical, electrical, agricultural, constructional and transport and highway engineering – the health services, and public and business administration, a choice of priorities which was to be confirmed later by the survey of *Requirements of Highly Trained Personnel* published by ICETEX in 1966. The universities were to co-ordinate their chosen sectors in order to avoid undue duplication of effort. At the same time recognition was given to the continued need for university participation in intermediate training to meet the country's requirements of technicians, in the manner of the National Polytechnic Institute in Mexico City. It recommended that universities should work along with independent technical colleges and polytechnics, still to be established, in making courses available both within the university precincts and extramurally, and that the qualifications for courses should be the same as for entry into the universities themselves. The courses might lead to higher technical certificates which would facilitate proceeding later to professional qualifications.

The short-term plan drew attention to the shortcomings in administration and organization of Colombian universities, which it described as out of date. Its proposals included sending specialists abroad for prolonged study of university administration. On return the specialists would work under the control of the Association to improve the administration of universities generally, and especially academic planning, student welfare, financial and office management, by means of seminars, short courses, consultation and discussion.

The short-term project was intended to cover the period ending in 1968, too short a term to allow some of the recommendations to be implemented, however well founded they may have been. Some have run into obstacles, and some have been overridden by events. The National University, for example, which during a century of existence had built up some twenty-six or more separate teaching units, including a few dispersed around the provinces, and an enrolment of twelve thousand, undertook a project of reorganization in 1965. It amalgamated its host of scattered units into eight faculties: Engineering, Science, Fine Arts, Social Sciences, Health, Agriculture, Education, and Philosophy and Letters. The purpose of the new alignment was modernization, coupled with administrative efficiency, but the changes were not brought about without teething troubles. Hopes disappointed, loss of status, sectional rivalries, administrative frustrations have absorbed the interest of everyone, and perhaps also the surplus energy of the student body. It is as yet, however, too early to judge whether the changes will settle the old problems of students' discord and unruliness, or improve the university's efficiency in dealing with the tasks thrust upon it by a developing country. For the moment no Colombian university can claim to have solved its problems. Few, if any, have a full complement of teachers, and though the Andes, and the universities at Tunja and Bucaramanga have made good progress in increasing the ratio of highly qualified staff, most still have serious teaching deficiencies, and many hardly merit higher education status.

The Association was certainly right in coming out against any increase in the number of universities, though this admonition seems to have gone unheeded and for reasons of provincial prestige Magdalena and Córdoba have been recognized indirectly. Whether it was right in envisaging a sharp increase in student population within the existing universities is still to be proved. Conscious effort to improve efficiency will no doubt ultimately eliminate bad management and overlap, though it is still possible to count some examples: there are four university departments of forestry but no centre for training forest workers. The disinterested observer would have the impression that already university expansion had gone beyond available human resources, and that while some should have a respite to re-form their forces, others should disappear, or at least be relegated to the secondary level.

A recently independent country such as Guyana has not entirely overlooked the fact that in some fields it is almost certainly cheaper to send students abroad for higher education to advanced countries where universities have already developed a range of higher studies impossible to match at home, apart from other considerations because of the prohibitive scale of capital expenditure involved. Of course, after independence it no longer seemed proper to depend entirely on overseas universities for the education of those who were to occupy the highest positions in the land, and the University of Guyana was founded as an important symbol of nationhood. Nevertheless, the overseas university remained a powerful attraction to students both because of its prestige and because of its facilities.

Colombia too has fully recognized the services foreign universities can offer to her development and has gone farther than most in organizing her programme of study abroad. The activities of ICETEX, and the researches into the needs for trained manpower carried out by this Institute have now laid the foundations for co-ordinating the higher education programmes at home and abroad. This bringing together of two patterns of thought about higher education is not before its time. The short-term plans for university development, calling for the acquisition of land, the erection and equipping of numerous buildings and the provision of expanded services, required a capital investment of 515 million pesos, and annual running costs of 1,800 million pesos. It was hoped that half of these sums would be made available from foreign sources, and that the public purse would supply 30 per cent of the requirements of the official universities. Already the hopes expressed in the plan were largely dashed by rising costs and it may now be doubtful whether the Colombian institutions will be able to meet the targets set for them. In any case at the moment, even though the National Council of Rectors continues to press the university's claim for more funds to maintain its growth, its contribution to technological progress and its academic standards, Colombia ranks not far behind Argentina, Uruguay and Venezuela in the proportion of the public budget for education allotted to the higher sector, without taking into account the considerable amounts derived by the private institutions from independent sources.

The short-term plan has now been superseded by a basic long-term plan for the development of higher education, formulated in 1967 by the Colombian Association of Universities with the collaboration of a team of experts from the University of California. The plan included a proposal to group the numerous universities of Colombia into regional clusters. In addition to the coastal group embracing Cartagena, Atlántico, Córdoba and Magdelena, which is being formed with north American help, four others were suggested. The north-western group would include the University of Caldas, and the section of the National University at Manizales, together with the Technological University of Pereira and the Universities of Quindio and Tolima. The Agricultural Faculty of the National University at Medellin would join with the Universities of Antioquia and Medellin, and the Bolivariana to form the Medellin group. The Santander group would include the Industrial University, the Polytechnic Institute of Bucaramanga, the University of Cucutá and the Rural Teachers' College at Pamplona. The fifth would be the national group, embracing the National University itself, and the two Pedagogical Universities at Bogotá and Tunja respectively. There would, in a manner of speaking, be five federal universities.

The plan aimed at some rationalization of the scattered faculties and schools which had grown up piecemeal over the whole country, just as within the National University there had been some amalgamation to form eight major faculties from the numerous separate schools and departments existing prior to 1965. It proposed to create a national university system which would have the advantage of the very large university without sacrificing the benefits of the small local university community. It would bring higher education equally to all parts of the country, in the same way as the Chilean regional colleges scheme, and at the same time avoid duplication of courses and administration. In order to achieve these ends the universities would make their entry requirements broadly the same everywhere, and would attempt some uniformity in the content and level of basic courses. Each university would develop its own special fields in the light of its resources and interests, but would not divert so far from a norm that students could not continue their specialization in another university. Examinations would be of equivalent standards and a system of 'credits' would make it possible for students to move from one university to another where facilities were more appropriate for the pursuit of the chosen speciality, and would make a wider choice available to students. Students would be able to transfer from one speciality to another within their own university if their abilities developed or their interests changed.

The plan could lead to considerable economy in the use of available resources and it might make possible a reduction in the incidence of student wastage, which amounts at the moment to half the enrolment. However, when the plan was published in 1967 it was too early to judge whether its assessment of problems and its recommentations would be generally accepted. By then it was already clear that to some even within the Association of Universities the proposals appeared to be an encroachment on academic freedom. Hardly any of the private universities liked it for this reason. Those that saw merit in it were in no position to further the plans because they had no independent resources to invest in regionalization, and they feared increased dependence on government funds would mean increased conformity to official thinking. For the time being, at any rate, the private institutions are outside the schemes.

Secondary schools

Sandwiched between the universities and the primary schools, the secondary school is indispensable to both. The healthy growth of the primary school depends above anything else on the secondary school producing an adequate stream of young people who will choose teaching as their vocation. The university is no less dependent on the secondary cycle for students adequately prepared for higher studies. In Colombia both are disappointed. Whereas in the field of higher education private establishments and an independent organization such as the Association of Universities have been in the forefront of the movement for reform and progress, there is no parallel at the secondary level. There are, it is true, some fine private secondary schools among which should be included the *Gymnasio Moderno* as well as some foreign-style institutions. However, the mushrooming of private academies during the last decade has not been motivated entirely by strong public spirit. The Association of Private Schools does nothing to identify itself with official plans, nor does it think in terms of the role of the secondary school in national development, but rather of the protection of the interests of its members. The private schools cannot match the broader outlook of the private universities. It is no doubt inevitable that without any public support these schools reflect the attitudes of those who pay for them, the parents, and on the whole they come from a section of society which is not over-anxious that the doors should be opened to those who lack the means of paying. Nor is the public sector adequate to take all who seek entry and to make good the loss to the nation of potential ability which is deprived of educational opportunity by economic stringency. Both town and country are affected by the relatively low priority given to secondary education in the Government's educational planning.

The town suffers particularly because the secondary system is not meeting the chronic shortage of technicians with middle-level qualifications in the expanding industries. In 1963 ICETEX made an effort to determine the educational structure of the Colombian work force. A total of 1,884 private firms and government agencies employing over fifty people were polled, covering 17·1 per cent of the active sector of the population outside agriculture. The results indicated that 36·2 per cent of the labour force consisted of unskilled labour, and another 24·4 per cent of skilled or semi-skilled craftsmen. Office clerks and sales personnel accounted for the same proportion as trained labour, leaving no more than 1·9 per cent of the total accounted for by semi-professionals and technicians. There are in fact four times as many administrators and managers as technicians. The problem is well recognized and the National Apprenticeship Scheme was set up precisely to provide a solution. The achievements of the industrial, agricultural and commercial branches of SENA, which have been described, are impressive, but they have not been enough. The intervention of the universities into this level of training is no more than a makeshift. Indeed, some Colombian educationists question whether this gap in human resources can be filled unless the Government modifies its priorities and invests more in the secondary system, so that the schools can offer an education adequate to the needs of modern society, and available to all who are able to benefit from it, and not only to those who aspire to call themselves 'doctor' rather than to dirty their hands in industry (Velez, 1964). It is not only industrial processes which are held up. Much useful work in industrial research units and universities is being impeded because there is no centre, such as is being created in Brazil, for training laboratory technicians.

Equally the rural areas suffer, partly for the same reasons but even more particularly because the improvement of the village primary school, so inferior to its urban counterpart, is impossible without a great increase in the supply of teachers from the secondary schools. This special problem apart, the dearth of secondary education in the country areas is a factor contributing to their cultural decline and to the flight of intelligent young people to the town. In both countryside and town the secondary system in its existing form is the bottleneck restricting opportunity, and, what is possibly more important, is the cause of mounting impatience at the slow pace of social change. The pressures are rising on government to give secondary education a higher ranking in the order of claims on public educational expenditure.

The old and the new worlds

In 1963 the Organization of American States requested the Institute of Economic and Social Development Studies of Paris to assess the progress made in education throughout Latin America. The Institute's conclusion was that the targets set at Punta del Este and at Bogotá were too ambitious, particularly at the primary and secondary levels. It stressed the need for better links between the different stages and branches of the educational systems, and for getting rid of the discrimination against rural education. A 20 per cent increase in higher education over five years was suggested, with the major part of students enrolment in the sciences and technology. A fundamental reform of educational administration and the training of a corps of professional administrators was judged to be a prerequisite of improvement. On the whole this evaluation fitted Colombia, though in the secondary sector Colombia's ambitions had been pitched somewhat lower than those of some neighbouring countries.

Like the rest of the Latin American continent, Colombia is in the throes of a struggle between the old and the future worlds. She has some advantageous attributes. Colombia has long belonged to the West where the individual could improve his portion if he chose the moment to do so. Indeed, the country was settled by the individual efforts of the *conquistadores* for whom the prospect of gold and land in plenty was a constant spur. She is more fortunate than her sister republic Peru in that, if her people are not entirely homogeneous, they do not feel themselves to be split racially. There is a considerable mixture of races, but a very small proportion can claim to be pure Negro, or Indian, or white. There are Negroes, particularly on the coast, and in practice there is some discrimination; there are also those who can trace pure descent directly from Europe, and though they have retained a good deal of power they have not monopoly of it as a racial group. Both groups are small. Generally speaking there are no large groups distinguished by racial or even cultural characteristics from the main body of the people. Particular fields of activity have not become the preserve of particular racial communities. A measure of the good fortune of this circumstance is given by the experience of Guyana, where communities of people of mainly African, Asian, or European origin have preserved some separate indentity and have recently come into violent conflict. One intractable problem was to redress the quasi-monopoly over the public services, and particularly over the police and the armed forces, exercised by people of African and mixed ancestry at the expense of those of Asian descent. Immigrants from India came to Guyana to replace the Africans who deserted the sugar plantations on emancipation. The Africans, or some of them, made the most of freedom and of elementary education, which became available during the second half of the nineteenth century, to get their feet on the lower rungs of the ladder of the civil service and of urban industrial employment. Only more recently have the Asians begun to stir, first by establishing a prominent position in the rural areas as rice farmers and landowners, and as professional and businessmen in the towns, and latterly in politics, trade unions and industry. The Asian also stands somewhat apart from the rest of the Guyanese by retaining more of the culture of his homeland than other groups, who have become assimilated to the Western world, and this intensifies the tensions which arise from the threat others see in the inroads into traditional preserves made by the East Indians.

The situation is further bedevilled by differences of religion, colour and class. In addition to numerous demoninations and sects of the Christian Church, there are Islamic and Hindu communities, and the two latter feel that, as a result of deliberate policy, at least by the former colonial authorities, they have not had a fair share of the resources available for establishing schools. Colour also, often working with social class, has created resentment. Here the African and the Asian may be allies against the European and the Chinese. There has been much miscegenation resulting in almost infinite gradations of pigmentation, and an almost equal number of focal points of envy and contumely. The considerable ethnic mixing which has occurred in Colombia, however, has not prevented a measure of homogeneity in outlook.

Colombia is also fortunate in that the conflict between the old and the new is possibly not so disrupting as in those areas of Africa and Asia and even other parts of South America in which the modern world of technology clashes with a more primitive civilization, and where, for example, the graduate engineer or scientist may have had his schooling in a remote bush village, still the home of parents who adhere to tribal ways. As he makes his way in the modern world, the educated Colombian is not enmeshed in an archaic family system, which places on him the obligation to share his material prosperity with countless relatives. Also Colombia has no major linguistic problems: a very fine Spanish is spoken universally, and the language of the home does not differ from the language of the schoolroom. And Colombia has a substantial body of middle-class urban dwellers who clearly constitute a reservoir of potential talent needed for modern development. Although some may have made use of modern techniques to build up personal wealth and to enjoy it more flamboyantly than would be seemly in Britain, there is nothing backward about them.

There is, however, also a legacy from the past which is not favourable to change. The society which persisted through four centuries of Colombia's colonial and post-colonial history was tradition-ruled, the people submitting without too much demur to the dominance of the priest and overlord. Perhaps also the memory of earlier pre-Colombian civilization, when the individual counted for nothing outside his role as a member of the community, conditioned the humble man to submissiveness to his lot. No doubt, too, exploitation and oppression over generations have contributed to the attitude of resigned hopelessness which has long been characteristic of the peasant and the labourer, and which is now a serious obstacle to progress. The human material available is not malleable enough to be easily forged, so to speak and where the readiness to change old-established attitudes does not exist, no amount of expertise from outside will achieve very much.

At the same time as the lack of ambition holds back advance, the polarity characteristic of Colombian and other Latin American societies leads to divided purposes and actual disturbances, which particularly disrupt the smooth evolution of the educational processes working for social change.

In Colombia as elsewhere a child's chances of surviving primary school and entering secondary are related to the socio-economic background of the parents. Evidence from places as diverse as Britain (Furneaux, 1961) and Chile (Hamuy, 1960) indicates that children from poor homes suffer considerable disadvantage. In the minds of many Colombians and other Latin Americans the failure to reach secondary school is to be attributed to the restriction of opportunity deliberately contrived by the oligarchs. It is true, of course, that modern communications, bringing news of material progress made by other societies open new vistas and persuade many to reject the inevitability of the extremes of wealth and poverty which still divide the favoured few from the masses. The messages of encouragement and the knowledge which come from abroad are increasingly vital factors contributing to technical and social advance. But the vision of improvement also intensifies the division of society, provoking resentment and tension. Should the frustrations become beyond bearing and lead to violence, the values and achievements built up with so much effort through the course of history are in jeopardy. There are individuals both cultured and patriotic who fear this destruction, and who would forestall it by holding in careful check the pace of change.

Public health officials are not noticeably agents of revolution, yet they are cutting down the time still left for leisurely choice. Under the protection of modern health services, the population increases relentlessly and economic development becomes less a means of improving living standards, and more a desperate urgency to feed new mouths. The population of Latin America is already greater than that of the United States, and is expected to reach three hundred and three million by 1975. The population of Colombia has reached eighteen millions and is expected to be twenty-two millions in another eight years, twice the inhabitants of the country in 1951. The birth-rate in Bogotá is 33·8 per thousand and the death-rate 19·6. Medellin is equally healthy, and more fertile with a birth-rate of over 41 per thousand. Half the population of the country is under fifteen years of age and will not contribute much to the production of goods for some time to come. The frightening rate of growth of population emphasizes the sheer magnitude of the problem. To meet the requirements of the continent in 1975 it has been estimated that South America will have to increase the internal production of machinery eighteen times, of steel seven times, of cars six times and of chemicals fourfold. This scale of production will require not simply a tremendous investment of human resources. The technological processes involved will demand an increasing number of qualified people to perform complex jobs, and the number of jobs simple enough to be performed by workers with little or no education relatively will decline. In the course of time the educational system must expand, and also become more complex and varied (CEPAL, *La Educación*, 1962). At the same time, the system will be called upon to prepare minds to accept great changes in social patterns and ways of thought, in spite of its links with the existing social structure and its tendency to be conservative.

Education, revolution and reform

This is the setting of Colombian educational expansion and reform. Some call for greater effort and speed, others see danger in precipitate action, taken often with insufficient resources and little statistical justification. The sort of society expected from the decisions being taken in the educational field is foreseen only obscurely. No clear answer can be given to the questions in many minds. Will the old pattern of life be destroyed? Will the emergence of new educated citizens make peaceful change possible? Or will two worlds continue to exist side by side, the one highly educated, the other at the opposite pole, ignorant and illiterate? Will universal education with enhanced national feeling bring also a blossoming of indigenous culture from the past, and the disappearance of European values which educated Colombians have nurtured for so long? Or will both be obliterated by the technological age? The only one of these ultimate ends which received specific mention in educational plans is the last, and then only to a limited extent in relation to the need to redress the conspicuous dearth of technical skills. It is the only objective whose outcome can be planned and foreseen in specific quotas of specialists. What the social effects of these cadres will be is interpreted in various ways, reflecting the outlook of the individual. There are those among the younger generation of students and intellectuals who think that no genuine contribution to a better world can be made by the present system of education under the aegis of the traditional ruling class. For them Che Guevara rightly advocated violence. Cuba's total social and political revolution, sweeping away the pretence of gradual and peaceful reform through education, seems the proper order of events and the way to make schools and universities serve the true needs of economic development. Quite another view of the benefits of messianic revolution is taken by the older middle-class generation, the ardours of reforming zeal of their youth now cooled by experience. Nor do they stand alone. Increasing numbers of young professionals, the university qualification in their pocket, make themselves a niche to defend in the modern sector of the economy. They find the new opportunities for a better life presented by the development of commerce and industry, and the peaceful revolution of education more convincing than the Cuban Utopia. Colombia, and all Latin America, carrying still the backwardness of the past, wait with impatience for the future to give the answer.

Bibliography

DE ALCAZAR, ANTONIO 1964 *Los Barí* Bogotá, Centro Capuchino de Historia

ASOCIACIÓN COLOMBIANA DE UNIVERSIDADES 1965 *Estudio sobre el Desarrollo Universitario a Corto Plazo* Bogotá, Asociación Colombiana de Universidades

1967 *Plan Basico de la Educación Superior 1968–75* Bogotá, Asociación Colombiana de Universidades

BALOGH, THOMAS 1965 *Problems and Strategies of Educational Planning: Lessons from Latin America* (Record of International Institute for Educational Planning Seminar 1964), Paris, Unesco, p. 26

BARDECI, O. J. and ESCONDRILLAS, E. 1963 *Financiamiento de la Educacion en America Latina* Washington, Pan American Union

BENJAMIN, HAROLD R. W. 1965 *Higher Education in Latin America* New York, McGraw Hill

BON, ISMAEL, RODRIGUEZ 1963 *La Educación Superior en America Latina* Washington, Pan American Union

BRITISH COUNCIL 1967 *Overseas Students in Britain* British Council

BURNS, H. W. 1963 'Social Class in Education in Latin America' *Comparative Education Review* Vol. 6, No. 3, p. 230

CALVERT, PETER 1967 'The Typical Latin American Revolution' *International Affairs*, Vol. 43, No. 1

CANO, CELERIMO 1964 'La Educación Primaria en Mexico' Washington, *La Educación*, Vol. IX, No. 33, p. 69

CEPAL 1962 'Desarrollo Económico y Educación en America Latina', Washington, *La Educación*, Nos. 25–26

DEBEAUVAIS, M. 1967 'The Development of Education in Latin America since the Santiago Plan' *World Yearbook of Education*

DEES, M. 1965 'Politics and Violence' *Encounter*, September 1965

FALS BORDA, ORLANDO 1961 'La Transformación de la America Latina y sus Implicaciones sociales y económicas' Bogotá, *LaNueva Economia*, Vol. 1, No. 2

FALS BORDA, ORLANDO 1965 'Violence and the Breakup of Tradition in Colombia' (contribution to *Obstacles to Change in Latin America*, ed. Claudio Velez) Oxford University Press

FINER, S. E. 1967 'Military and Society in Latin America' *Sociological Review*, No. 11

166

Bibliography

FITZGERALD, DEAN T. 1957 'The significance of American Schools in Latin America' *Comparative Education Review*, Vol. 1, No. 2

FURNEAUX, W. D. 1961 *The Chosen Few* Oxford University Press for Nuffield Foundation

GHIOLDI, ALFREDO 1964 'La Escuela Primaria en la Argentina' Washington, *La Educación*, Vol. IX, No. 33, p. 29

GOMEZ VALDERRAMA, PEDRO 1964 *Memoria del Ministro de Educación* (1963) Vol. 1; Vol. 2. *El Desarrollo Educativo* Bogotá, Colombian Ministry of Education

GRIFFIN, CHARLES C. 1961 *Latin America and the Enlightenment* (ed. A. P. Whitaker) New York, Cornell University Press

GUYANA GOVERNMENT 1966 *Development Plan 1962–72* Georgetown, Government of Guyana Printery

GUZMAN, GERMAN 1967 *Camilo: Presencia y Destino* Bogotá, Servicios Especiales de Prensa

GUZMAN, GERMAN and UNAÑA LUNA, EDUARDO, and FALS BORDA, ORLANDO 1962, 1964 *La Violencia en Colombia* 2 Vols. Bogotá, Tercer Mundo

HAMUY, EDUARDO 1960 *Educación Elemental, Analfabetismo y desarrollo Económico* Santiago de Chile, Editorial Universitaria

HAVIGHURST, ROBERT J. 1961 'Latin America and Higher Education' *Comparative Education Review*, Vol. 4, No. 3, p. 174

HAVIGHURST, ROBERT J., and ABREU, JAIME 1962 'The Problems of Secondary Education in Latin America' *Comparative Education Review*, Vol. 5, No. 3, p. 167

HARBISON, F., and MYERS, CHARLES A. 1964 *Education, Manpower and Economic Growth* New York, McGraw

HJELM, HOWARD J. 1963 *Alliance for Progress and Education in Latin America* Washington, Pan American Union

ICETEX 1966 *Resources and Requirements for Highly-trained Personnel* Bogotá, Instituto Colombiano de Especialización Técnica en el Exterior

JAMES, W. S. 1959 Address to British Guiana Teachers' Association unpublished

LARREA, J. 1963 'Random Thoughts on the Economic Basis for Education in Latin America' *Comparative Education Review*, Vol. 7, No. 2, p. 162

LOURENCO-FILHO, M. B. 1964 'Relaciones entre la Enseñanza Primaria y la Enseñanza Media en America Latina' Washington *La Educación*, Vol. IX, No. 33, p. 5

LOURENCO-FILHO, M. B. 1965 'The Explosion of Education in Latin America' *World Yearbook of Education*

Bibliography

MADARIAGA, SALVADOR DE 1947 *The Fall of the Spanish Empire* Hollis and Carter

MASCARO, CARLOS C. 1964 'Administración de la Washington Educación en America Latina' *La Educación*, Vol. IX, No. 33, p. 83

MASON, J. ALDEN, 1957 *The Ancient Civilization of Peru* Penguin Books

MEDINA, RAFAEL BERNAL 1966 'Educational Relations between Church and Government in Colombia' *World Yearbook of Education*

NITSCH, MANFRED 1964 'Fundamental Integral Education: Radio Schools in Latin America' *Comparative Education Review*, Vol. 8, p. 340

PAN AMERICAN UNION 1955 *Recommendaciones aprobadas por el Seminario Inter-americano de la Educación Secondaria: Santiago de Chile 1954–55* Washington, Pan American Union

PELAEZ, LEON CORTINAS 1963 'Autonomy and Student Co-Government' *Comparative Education Review*, Vol. 7, No. 2, p. 166

PIKE, F. and BRAY, D. 1960 'A Victim of Catastrophe: the Future of Chile – U.S. Relations' *Review of Politics*

PINHEIRO, LUCIA, MARQUES 1964 'Programas y Técnicas de Enseñanza Primaria en Brasil: Experiencias Recientes' Washington, *La Educación*, Vol. IX, No. 33, p. 45

POSADA, JAIME 1962 *Una Política Educativa* Bogotá, Colombia Ministry of Education

REYES, CARMONA, MARCO F. 1965 *Estudio Socio-Económico del Fenómeno de la Immigración a Bogotá* Bogotá, Económica Colombiana

SOUSTELLE, J. 1961 *The Daily Life of the Aztecs* Weidenfeld and Nicolson

TORRES RESTREPO, C., CORREDOR RODRIGUEZ, B. 1961, *Las Escuelas Radiofonicas de Sutatenza – Colombia* Bogotá, Centro de Investigaciones Sociales

UNESCO 1960 *La Situación Educativa en America Latina*; 1963, *La Educación Primaria en America Latina*; 1965, *Problems and Strategies of Educational Planning Lessons from Latin America* (Record of International Institute for Educational Planning Seminar 1964), Paris, Unesco

VELEZ GARCIA, JORGE 1964 *Características de la Educación en Colombia durante el ultimo deceno* Bogotá, Colombian Ministry of Education

WOLFE, MARSHALL 1965 Article in *Problems and Paris Strategies of Educational Planning* (see above), Unesco

Further reading

ANDERSON, CHARLES W. 1967 *Politics and Economic Change in Latin America* Princeton, New Jersey, Van Nostrand. Political factors are emphasized in this description of economic and social change. The author concludes that Latin America will evolve its own solutions without cataclysmic upheaval.

BLAKEMORE, H. 1966 *Latin America* Oxford University Press (Modern World Series). After describing the people and history of Latin America the author indicates the changes the continent is now facing. He poses the question 'revolution or evolution?' and stresses the importance of the answer for the contemporary world.

HALMOS, PAUL (ed.) 1967 'Latin American Sociological Studies', (*The Sociological Review*, Monograph 11) University of Keele. This series of essays emphasizes the persistence of traditional values and problems in the face of factors making for change. Particular attention is paid to the political implications of population growth, and to instability and violence.

HARBISON, F., and MYERS, CHAS. A. *Education, Manpower and Economic Growth* New York, McGraw, Hill. An analysis of the educational priorities called for at different stages of economic growth. An attempt is made to classify countries in terms of human resources development as under-developed, partially developed, semi-advanced or advanced.

MASON, J. ALDEN 1957 *The Ancient Civilization of Peru* Penguin Books. An account of the legends surrounding the growth of the Inca Empire and of the economic, social and political life which flourished on the plateaux of Peru on the arrival of the Spaniards.

SOUSTELLE, JACQUES 1961 *The Daily Life of the Aztecs* Weidenfeld and Nicolson. This translation from French describes every aspect of the high level of civilization reached by Aztec society before the arrival of the Spaniards.

VELEZ, CLAUDIO (ed.) 1965 *Obstacles to Change in Latin America* Oxford University Press (under auspices of Royal Institute for International

Affairs). A collection of essays by leading Latin Americans who are both academics and also involved in planning. A distinctively Latin American view.

Education

BENJAMIN, HAROLD R. W. 1965 *Higher Education in the American Republics* New York, McGraw, Hill. A description of the history and present characteristics of American universities. The objectives, programmes, organization and finance, and the teaching and student bodies are analysed in the five main areas into which the continents are divided: the southern Spanish countries, the Caribbean, Central America and Mexico, Brazil and the U.S.A.

GUYANA GOVERNMENT 1968 *Memorandum on Educational Policy* Georgetown, Guyana Government Printery. A brief statement.

LYONS, RAYMOND F. (ed.) 1965 *Problems and Strategies of Educational Planning Lessons from Latin America* Paris, Unesco and International Institute for Educational Planning. A record of a seminar held in Paris in 1964 which brought together educators, sociologists and political scientists from Latin America, U.S.A. and Europe. One group of papers deals with the social, political and economic setting. Another group describes what has been achieved to date, while a final section identifies some of the major challenges to educational planning, including rural educational policies and the problem of regional cooperation at the university level.

MYERS, CHAS. N. 1965 *Education and National Development in Mexico* Princeton, Princeton University. A regional analysis of the relationship between education and economic growth which brings out the disparity of educational provision between backward rural areas and advanced urbanizations. The immediate elimination of backward areas might have to be put aside, it is suggested, in the interests of rapid national growth, which must come before local problems can be solved.

PAN AMERICAN UNION 1963 *La Educación Primaria en America Latina* Washington, Organization of American States (for Unesco). A survey of the first stage of education covering the extent of compulsory provision, the training and status of teachers, curricula and methods, and administration and finance. There are sections dealing with the place of the primary school in the whole educational system, and in relation to the demo-graphic, economic and social situation. Appendices also cover enrolment, school libraries, equipment and standards.

UNESCO 1962 'Proyecto Principal de Educación' (*Boletín trimestral*, No. 13) Paris, Unesco. Papers dealing with the demographic, economic, social and educational situation in Latin America prepared in connection with the Conference on Education and Economic and Social Develop-ment held in Santiago, Chile, in 1962. An extensive bibliography is included.

Index

Administration of education 15 et seq
 advisory councils 16, 17
 by the State 16, 42, 47, 78, 79, 112, 147
 local authorities 16, 17
Adult education and community development 18, 21, 22, 37, 101, 107 et seq
 agricultural extension 121
 community and basic education 118 et seq, 128
 CREFAL (Fundamental Education Centre for Latin America, Rubio) 36, 37 et seq, 44, 109, 112, 117, 120
 finance 120
 radio schools 123 et seq
  Latin American Federation of Radio Schools 126
  Radio Sutatenza and Acción Cultural Popular (Colombia) 101, 123 et seq, 130, 145
 Universidad Obrera, Cali, Colombia, 101, 118
Agricultural education 18, 21, 55, 69, 121, 128, 129, 154
 faculties of agriculture 129
 see also adult education and rural education
Alliance for Progress 19, 20, 22, 23, 33, 110, 111, 114, 135, 146, 148
Amerindians 3, 7, 12, 117, 161
 Araucanian 6
 Aztec 6, 7
 Barí 7
 Guaraní 7
 Inca 6, 7, 8
 Quechua 6, 7, 117
Argentina 5, 6, 11, 14, 25, 26, 27, 29, 30, 43, 44, 45, 46, 47, 48, 60, 64, 65, 75, 76, 77, 81, 82, 83, 84, 85, 87, 92, 93, 97, 104, 105, 117, 149, 150, 156
Aztec (see Amerindians)

Basic education (see adult education)
Belgium 138, 145
Bogotá 3, 4, 8, 9, 10, 22, 23, 36, 37, 66, 93, 98, 109, 111, 119, 132, 143, 150, 157, 160, 164
Bolivia 5, 26, 30, 43, 65, 81, 82, 87, 93, 99, 104, 106, 107, 117, 126, 149
Brain drain 144
Brasilia 94
Brazil 3, 4, 5, 6, 7, 12, 14, 17, 23, 24, 25, 26, 27, 35, 39, 43, 46, 47, 48, 49, 53, 57, 60, 62, 64, 70, 81, 82, 83, 84, 87, 92, 93, 104, 105, 106, 108, 138, 142, 149
 national fund for secondary education 26, 48
Buenos Aires 11, 110

Cambridge Overseas Certificate 49
Canada 76
Capuchin 8
Caracas 11, 95, 102
CARE (Cooperative for American Relief Everywhere) 32, 121
Caro y Cuervo, Instituto 76, 141
Castro, Fidel 102, 107
 'fidelismo' 103, 104, 107
Central American Common Market 92
CEPAL (Comisión Económica para America Latina) 164
Chile 5, 6, 11, 14, 26, 27, 29, 39, 40, 43, 46, 47, 60, 64, 65, 75, 76, 79, 81, 82, 83, 84, 93, 95, 101, 104, 107, 110, 114, 126, 149, 150, 157, 163

Chinese 6, 162

Church

Roman Catholic 7, 10, 13, 14 et seq, 18, 48, 58, 65, 67, 75, 78, 82, 91, 93, 97 et seq, 124 et seq

and military 106

others 161, 162

Ciudad Guyana 95

CIES (Inter-American Economic and Social Council) 109

Coffee Growers, Colombian Association of 38, 122, 140

Colombia 3 et seq, 6, 7, 9, 10, 12, 14, 16, 18, 19, 22, 23, 24, 25, 26, 27, 29, 31, 32, 34, 36, 37, 39, 40, 41, 42, 43, 44, 46, 48, 50, 53, 54, 55, 59, 60, 61, 63, 64, 65, 68, 74, 75, 76, 78, 79, 81, 82, 83, 84, 85, 87, 92, 93, 96, 97, 100, 104 et seq, 107, 110, 118, 119, 123 et seq, 129, 132, 135, 137, 142, 145, 147 et seq, 156, 158, 160, 162

Communications 13, 92

Community development (*see* adult education)

Conferences, Inter-American 16, 19, 20, 22, 23, 24, 35, 36, 50, 107, 109, 110, 112, 113

of Latin-American Educators 108

Regional Conference of Latin American States on Free and Compulsory Education, Lima 20, 110

on Integral Planning of Education 19, 111

2nd Conference of Education Ministers 20, 110, 147

3rd Conference of Education Ministers 22, 23, 111

on Secondary Education, Santiago de Chile 110 et seq

Constitutions 5, 14 et seq, 23, 48

Costa Rica 5, 6, 24, 26, 27, 64, 75, 83, 149

CREFAL (Fundamental Education Centre for Latin America) (*see* adult education)

Cuba 99, 101, 102, 103, 104, 107, 114, 149, 165

Curricula 16, 17 et seq, 21, 34, 35, 40, 49 et seq

See also under various branches of education

Denmark 145

Dominican friars 65

Dominican Republic 12, 27, 43, 65, 149

Economic development 5, 19, 21, 22, 50, 119, 143, 149, 150

Ecuador 5, 6, 11, 24, 27, 36, 43, 44, 64, 65, 83, 93, 104, 110, 126, 149

'Educación, La' 36, 113 et seq, 130, 164

Educational Planning 19, 20 et seq, 23, 31, 32, 61, 69, 76, 110, 141, 147, 148, 149, 150, 153, 159, 160, 164 et seq
– financial planning 23 et seq

Exchange of Students for Technical Experience, International Association for 141

Experiment in International Living 141

El Salvador 15, 46, 75

Europe 5, 6, 8, 92, 131, 136, 150, 161, 162, 165

Financing of education 20, 22, 23 et seq, 31, 32, 55, 79 et seq, 99 et seq, 120, 140, 148, 152, 156, 159, 160

Ford Foundation 52, 80

France 3, 8, 56, 131, 132, 133, 136, 137, 138, 139

Free schools 18, 48

Germany 6, 56, 76, 131, 132, 133, 136, 137, 138, 139, 145

Girls, education of 59, 73 et seq

Guatamala 5, 30, 43, 82, 92, 149

Guevara, Che 99, 165

Guyana 4, 6, 13, 15, 31, 32, 33, 34, 39, 43, 45, 47, 48, 49, 50, 54, 61, 69, 70, 95, 133, 136, 150, 151, 156, 161

Haiti 26, 30
Higher education 17, 152 et seq
  see also universities
Honduras 5, 6, 12, 29, 36, 44, 75, 81, 92, 110, 117
Huachipato 95

ICETEX (Instituto Colombiano de Especialización Técnica en el Exterior) 23, 57, 63, 69, 83, 137 et seq, 147, 148, 154, 156, 159
ILCA (Instituto Lingüístico Colombo-Americano) 140
Illiteracy (*see* literacy)
Inca (*see* Amerindians)
India 6
Industry 7, 10, 11, 96, 97, 151
Inspectorates 17, 19
Instituto Peruano de Fomento Educativo 143
Institutos de Crédito y Fomento Educativo, Asociación Latino-Americano de 143
Inter-American Cultural Council 109
Inter-American Development Bank 146
International experts 134 et seq
Israel 131, 138
Italy 6, 131, 138

Japan 29, 138
Jesuits 7, 41, 47, 65, 66
  expulsion from Brazil 66
    Spanish dominions 66

Kellog Foundation 80

LAFTA (Latin American Free Trade Association) 92
Lancastrian schools 28, 39
La Paz 8
Las Casas 7
Lima 20, 126
Literacy 7, 12, 18, 19, 22, 31, 37, 96, 103, 117, 118, 119, 126, 127, 148, 150, 151, 152

Manpower and education 141 et seq, 144, 151, 152, 156, 159
Mexico 6, 7, 10, 14, 15, 17, 18, 19, 25, 26, 27, 29, 32, 40, 42, 43, 46, 48, 61, 64, 65, 70, 72, 82, 83, 85, 87, 92, 93, 103, 104, 107, 109, 117, 118, 126, 149, 150
Military forces 21, 28, 67
Military régimes 105 et seq

Negro 7, 161
Netherlands 121, 138, 145
Nicaragua 5, 26, 30, 36, 43, 44, 75, 110
Norway 76
Núcleo escolar (*see* rural education)

Organisation of American States 20, 44, 75, 109 et seq, 112, 113, 128, 134, 160
Overseas aid 13, 19, 123, 128, 131 et seq, 151, 157
  evaluation 144 et seq
  international experts 134 et seq
  study overseas 136 et seq, 142, 143, 144, 154, 156

Panama 24, 27, 43, 100
Pan American Union (*see* Organisation of American States)
Paraguay 5, 6, 27, 64, 79, 93, 104, 106, 149
Peace Corps (*see* U.S.A.)
Peru 3, 5, 6, 14, 16, 24, 25, 27, 39, 40, 57, 64, 65, 77, 82, 83, 84, 87, 93, 97, 104, 105, 110, 126, 145, 149, 160, 161
Political Parties 101
  Chile 101
  Colombia 9, 15, 19, 82, 101, 104 et seq
  Mexico 103
  Venezuela 102
Population 10, 11, 20, 27, 50, 93, 112, 119, 163 et seq
  family planning 93 et seq

Portugal 6
  Portuguese language 13, 17, 91
Primary schools 4, 7, 10, 12, 14, 17,
  18, 20, 22, 25, 26, 28 et seq, 96, 124,
  128, 148, 149, 153, 160, 163
  attendance 30 et seq, 129, 150
  buildings 32 et seq, 151
  curriculum 21, 34, 35
  enrolment 29 et seq, 32
  length of course 29, 34, 129
  model schools 35, 36, 39
  objectives 28
  radio and television 39 et seq
  single teacher schools 36
  size of classes 21, 29, 32, 37, 41
  standards 34 et seq
  teachers 41 et seq, 69, 107
  universal provision 14, 20, 31, 34,
    35, 41, 150
Punta del Este 111, 160

Quito 8, 60, 92
Quechua (*see* Amerindians)

Radio and television 39 et seq, 61 et
  seq, 123 et seq
  Latin American Federation of Radio
    Schools 126
Rio de Janeiro 3, 17, 78
Rockefeller Foundation 80
Rural development 11, 22, 97, 119,
  127 et seq
  Banco Cafetero, Colombia 122
  Cája Agraria, Colombia 122, 128
  INCORA (Colombian Institute for
    Agricultural Reform) 122, 128
Rural education 25, 34, 36 et seq, 121,
  124, 160
  CREFAL, Rubio (Latin American
    Fundamental Education Centre)
    (*see* adult education)
  núcleo escolar 37 et seq, 120, 127,
    129
  see also adult education

Santiago de Chile 16, 20, 23, 24, 27,
  50, 110
  declaration of 21

São Paulo 3, 11, 17, 110
Secondary schools 12, 14, 15, 17, 18,
  20, 21, 22, 25, 26, 44, 46 et seq, 55,
  110, 131 et seq, 142, 148, 153, 154,
  158 et seq, 160, 163
  attendance 22, 59
  'bachillerato' 50, 58, 60, 63, 84, 153
  'bachillerato nocturno' 52
  comprehensive schools 50, 52
  curriculum 49 et seq, 110, 132
  enrolment 46, 58
  for girls 59
  model schools 51
  objectives 63
  pilot project 51 et seq
  private schools 18, 26, 47, 58, 59,
    131 et seq, 158 et seq
  radio and television 61 et seq
  reform 50 et seq, 110
  research 51
  science 60
  school buses 59
  shift system 58
  state schools 48, 59, 159
  teachers 53, 60 et seq, 132
    – status 61, 108
  vocational schools 53 et seq
SENA (*see* vocational education)
Southern Association of Colleges and
  Schools (U.S.A.) 85
Spain 6, 7, 9, 56, 66, 131, 137, 138
  Spanish language 6, 13, 14, 35, 40,
    50, 91, 117, 126, 141, 161, 162
Student Travel, Council on 141
Switzerland 3, 138, 145

Teachers 12, 18, 21, 24, 25, 28, 31,
  40, 41 et seq, 49, 53, 58, 60 et seq, 120,
  129, 132, 133, 147, 148
  Conference of Latin American
    Educators 108
  influence 107 et seq
  status of 45, 61, 108
  Teachers' Association (Argentina)
    44
Teacher training 17, 18, 21, 27, 34,
  35, 42 et seq, 52, 53, 69, 151

Teacher training *(contd.)*
Felix Bernasconi Insitute (Argentina) 44
Instituto Federal de Capacitación del Magisterio (Mexico) 43
Instituto Nacional de Capacitación y Perfeccionamiento (Colombia) 43
Teachers Training College (Guyana) 43
National Institute for Pedagogical Studies (Brazil) 35
model colleges
    Pamplona 36, 120, 157
    Teguciagalpa 36
    Jinopete 36
    San Pablo
normal schools 42 et seq
Technology 11, 91 et seq, 104, 105, 112, 137, 144, 163, 164
technicians 11, 142, 154, 159, 160
Television *(see* radio)
Textbooks 18, 21, 35, 124
Torres, Camilo 97 et seq

UNESCO 20, 29, 30, 35, 36, 41, 42, 44, 110, 112, 117, 134, 138
Universities 12, 21, 65 et seq, 131, 155, 160
Argentina 65, 66, 75, 76, 77, 81, 83, 84, 85, 87
Bolivia 65, 68, 70, 81, 87
of Bologna 78
Brazil 35, 77, 81, 83, 84, 87
    Colegios de Aplicão 60, 67
Chile 35, 65, 66, 72, 75, 76, 77, 79, 81, 82, 83, 84, 157
Colombia 23, 35, 41, 51, 52, 65, 66, 67, 68, 70, 74, 75, 76, 78, 80, 81, 82, 83, 84, 85, 87, 98, 101, 118, 119, 120, 129, 140, 142, 152 et seq, 154, 157
    Association of Universities 18, 23, 75, 80, 83, 85, 86, 87, 138, 140, 147, 148, 152, 153, 154, 155, 157, 158
    Seminar of faculties of education 60

Costa Rica 25, 83
Cuba 83
Ecuador 65, 83
El Salvador 75
Guatamala 75
Guyana 69, 136, 156
Honduras 75, 81
Mexico 40, 65, 70, 72, 73, 74, 80, 83, 85, 87, 103, 154
Nicaragua 75
Paraguay 79
Peru 65, 66, 77, 78, 81, 82, 83, 84, 87
Santo Domingo 65
Uruguay 67, 79, 81, 83, 85
U.S.A. 75, 85, 87, 140, 157
Venezuela 65, 76, 81, 83
West Indies 69, 85
academic freedom 77
enrolment 69, 82 et seq, 84, 153, 160
entry tests 154
finance 79 et seq, 152, 156
foundations, North American 79
libraries 72, 85, 129, 154
Manifesto of the Youth of Cordoba 77
organization 72, 78, 154 et seq
reform 77 et seq
research 35 et seq, 76 et seq, 160
service to community 73 et seq, 153
standards 84 et seq
students 11, 77, 80 et seq, 87, 98, 105, 106, 107, 108, 120, 147, 152 et seq, 158
    Continental Latin American Students Association 99
    social origin 49, 82, 87, 137, 154, 163
teachers 86 et seq, 108, 152, 154, 155
television 73
women 73
University curricula 67, 72, 154
agriculture 69, 74, 129, 155
'credits' 72, 158

University curricula *(contd.)*
  education 17, 51, 60, 67, 69
  fine arts, 155
  languages 71
  law 68, 69
  liberal studies 70
  medicine 68, 69, 155
  professional studies 67, 72, 73, 154
  science 155
  social sciences 68, 69, 74, 75, 155
  technical studies 67, 68, 69, 74, 155, 160
United Kingdom 8, 56, 94, 133, 138, 139, 145, 161, 163
Urbanization 10 et seq, 13, 37, 96 et seq, 150, 151, 157
Uruguay 5, 10, 27, 36, 43, 46, 47, 64, 67, 79, 81, 83, 85, 93, 106, 117, 149, 150, 156
U.S.A. 24, 29, 56, 75, 76, 85, 87, 114, 122, 123, 128, 131, 132, 134, 135, 137, 138, 139, 140, 144
  Agency for International Development 40, 75
  peace corps 40, 121, 122, 144, 145, 150, 151

Venezuela 11, 17, 24, 25, 27, 31, 36, 42, 43, 44, 47, 64, 65, 66, 81, 82, 83, 93, 94, 97, 102, 104, 107, 110, 126, 149, 150, 156
Violence 9 et seq, 13, 22, 23, 91, 97, 106, 119, 150, 163
Vocational Education 11, 53 et seq, 70, 96
  agriculture 62
  commercial education 62, 57
  'Escuela de Práctico Agropecuarios' 53
  'Politécnicos complementarios' 53
  SENA (National Apprenticeship Service) (Col.) 54 et seq, 63, 145, 147, 148, 159
  SENA (Industrial Apprenticeship Service Brazil) 57
  SENAC (Commercial Apprenticeship Service Brazil) 57
  SENATI (National Apprenticeship Service Peru) 57, 145
    technical education 53 et seq, 62, 154
    at university level *(see* universities)

Young Farmers Clubs 121, 122

Printed and bound by CPI Group (UK) Ltd, Croydon, CR0 4YY

01/05/2025

01858435-0001